Beautiful
North
Norfolk

Terry Palmer

A Heritage House Publication

BEAUTIFUL NORTH NORFOLK
First published May 2005
ISBN 1.815215.0793

Printed by Hythe Offset, Colchester
Published by Heritage House (Publishers) Ltd
Steam Mill Road, Bradfield, Manningtree, CO11 2QT
w.w.w.heritage-house.co.uk
e-mail: sales@heritage-house.co.uk

Heritage House publishes a range of **Ordnance Survey scale-linked**
walkers' maps and street plans to various tourist areas of East Anglia,
including a walker's map of the immediate area to accompany this book.
Their scale is constant for each map and currently they cover these
areas: Peddar's Way, Wells to Weybourne, Weybourne to Cromer.

Photo Beans Seal Trips ©Adrian Judd Eastern Daily Press
Cromer Lifeboat ©"Poppyland Photos"

Cover: Attractions in North Norfolk

Also by Terry Palmer:

The Cairo Alternative	A Day Out In Aldeburgh
A Day Out In Blakeney	A Day Out In The New Forest
A Day Out In Southwold	Discover Cyprus & North Cyprus
Discover Florida	Discover The Gambia
Discover Gibraltar	Discover Guernsey Alderney Sark
Discover The Isle Of Man	Discover Jersey
Discover Malta	Discover Morocco
Discover The Suffolk Coast	Discover Tunisia
Discover Turkey	Euroslavia
The Ghost At My Shoulder	I've Been Here *Before*
Naked Came I	

CONTENTS

Holkham Hall

BEAUTIFUL NORTH NORFOLK
INFRASTRUCTURE AND SUPERSTRUCTURE

NORTH NORFOLK *is* beautiful – no kidding! Look at the quaint roads, the flint cottages, the peaceful harbours. Why else do people buy up holiday homes and – elsewhere in the county – crowd into the Broads each summer, and overflow the beaches at Great Yarmouth?

Norfolk itself is such a big county – 2,069 square miles with 800,000 people (2001) – that it can absorb all this and still leave vast, open, almost empty spaces in Breckland, and a scattering of tiny villages right across the landscape. At this stage we'd better acknowledge that boating on the Broads has peaked, the next land you come to if you go due north from Cromer is eastern Siberia, and Yarmouth is outside the scope of this book. No matter: we shall be looking at the northern coastal strip only.

Norfolk as an entity is one of the driest parts of England – Clacton in Essex is *the* driest – which means it gets plenty of sunshine. It also has the least altitude of all the counties (after the 1974 boundary changes), with Brink Hill near Great Massingham reaching the dizzy heights of 305 feet (93 metres if you're into metric). But it certainly isn't flat: there's a slope near Sandringham which reaches the gradient of 1:10 and makes cyclists think about walking.

And then there are those picturesque dumpy little hills along the coast behind Sheringham and Cromer. Would you believe it – they're *terminal moraines*. "What are they?" you may ask if geology isn't up your street. When the glaciers coming south over what is now the North Sea, umpteen years ago, met the higher land of Norfolk, they stopped, melted, and dropped all their rocks, soil, sand and other muck that they had brought from 'way up north. And it's still there today: one tump is even called Muckleburgh Hill, as we shall see much later.

Geology has played wonders with the coastline of East Anglia. From **Hunstanton** east to **Weybourne** the sea has swept down straight at the shore and piled up millions of tons of sand, giving those splendid beaches. From **Weybourne** right round to **Walton**-nearly-on-the-**Naze** (it's eroding) in Essex the current has swept along the littoral, polishing it as cleanly as a baby's bottom and carting away many more millions of tons of sand and gravel, which now lie in Orford Ness, Landguard Point off Felixstowe, and Foulness, as well as building up the Goodwin Sands.

History has also left its mark on the Norfolk landscape. If you can find a large-scale map of the middle of the county you can judge for yourself how extremely important **Walsingham** was in the Middle Ages. It was called England's Nazareth, a pilgrimage site, as holy in its time as Lourdes, Jerusalem, Knock, Fâtima and Santiago de Compostela have been in their times. Pilgrims came from all over England, and even from the nearby Continent, and they left their tracks which are still visible today. Many devout people walked, or rode donkeys, up from the south, while others came by boat to King's Lynn and Wells – and their routes to Walsingham can so easily be traced today as footpaths, bridle ways, and even tarred roads. Because footpaths have often been preserved as roads there are relatively few remaining purely as tracks, compared with other counties.

Among the major paths is **Peddar's Way**, from mid-Suffolk to Holme next the Sea near Hunstanton, built by the Romans in a dead straight line and with an extension in Lincolnshire going to Lincoln itself. From Holme the more modern **Norfolk Coast Path** meanders to Cromer along splendid if undramatic scenery, and at Cromer the **Weavers' Way** takes walkers on a circuitous route to Great Yarmouth, from where the **Angles' Way,** also called the **Waveney Way** leads back to Diss.

History has left its mark in other ways. Norwich was once the second most important city in England, and the county's population was bursting at the seams. That was before that other Industrial Revolution, when wool was king and East Anglia was its kingdom. Every community had its flocks of sheep and most of the cottages were pulsing with energy as the countryfolk sheared, carded, spun and wove their fibres. England had a thriving export trade in wool, and it has even left its mark on the language: do you go wool-gathering? Are you on tenterhooks? Have you ever been fleeced? The House of Lords still has its Woolsack, and there are wayside inns – alright, we call them pubs today – with names such as the Leg of Mutton, the Fleece, and even the Woolsack again. And there's a village in Suffolk called Woolpit.

6

But Time waits for no man. Wool gave way to cotton and most of Norfolk's villages shrank. As the housing stock of the day was mostly built of wattle and daub – lath covered in mud – with thatched roofs and beaten earth floors, it took only a few years for fire and rain to remove all signs. In far too many instances all that was left was the village church: which is why Norfolk today is a county dominated by its beautiful or bizarre, but always ancient, churches. And our little strip along the north coast has its ration of them.

CHURCHES

We have to blame the **Saxons** for a good many of our churches. In the county as a whole, **119** of them have round towers, an almost sure sign of their Saxon origins for they were built of flint, and you cannot raise a corner in this irregular material. The only other material the old-time masons had for use was **carrstone**, that reddish-brown rock found in Hunstanton cliffs, but as transport was terrible a thousand years ago, and flint is found almost everywhere in the county (except the Broads and Fens), that settled the issue. To strike a balance there are just 41 round towers in Suffolk, and only 14 elsewhere in Britain. I grant you that a few round towers were built after the Norman Conquest, but this era saw an increase in the use of water transport and from now on dressed corner stones made of limestone were shipped in from the north of France – it was still easier than hauling them from Leicestershire.

The TOWER evolved as a general-purpose feature. You could hang a bell in it and so summon the people to worship or to warn them of marauders; you could see those marauders much better; you provided a landmark for travellers, especially fishermen; you created a store for grain out of the reach of rats – and a tower was certainly a homage to God. There are so many churches in the county that it is difficult not to be in sight of at least one, and on our strip of the coast you can see Cley, Wiveton, Blakeney and Glandford churches from one vantage point. I leave you to find it.

The NAVE is the main part of the building, its roof often looking like an upturned boat, hence the naval link. Indeed, the word comes from the latin *navalis*. It is invariably built east-west, with the tower at the western end, though the tower may be freestanding, offset, or even in the middle of the building if the architect was clever. The east end of the nave usually held the CHAPEL, before the 16th-century Reformation built and maintained by the priest who had his own private entrance; the churchwardens were responsible for the rest of the building and had to use the public door.

Between nave and chapel was the ROOD BEAM, a sturdy timber 10 to 15 feet up, carrying the ROOD SCREEN, usually gaily carved. The ROOD itself was the carving of the crucified Christ and the subject of medieval oaths when people swore "by the rood". No church kept its rood intact after the Reformation, when Henry VIII became a 'protestant' against the Catholic Church, although you may still find traces of the rood stair set into an outer wall.

It was normal practice to enter the church via the SOUTH PORCH, on the sunny side, while the door in the NORTH PORCH was left open during baptisms for the Devil to escape. Modern road systems sometimes upset this tradition, but of Norfolk's 660 churches, 468 still use the south door, 152 the north, while 40 have a west door, usually through the tower.

The EAST WINDOW is the main source of light above the high altar and often has the best stained glass.

Even TOMBS have their own coded language. The carving of a man with crossed arms or legs tells us that he was wealthy enough to have made a pilgrimage to the Holy Land, but a man whose feet rested on a little dog had died peacefully at home. Sorry, ladies, but women had to have been *very* important before they were remembered in stone.

YEW TREES have been planted in churchyards since the coming of Christianity, not only as a reliable source of timber for archery, but we are only now learning their symbolism. However, a 1,200-year-old yew can usually pinpoint the site of a Saxon church even if no other trace of the building remains.

The church at Harpley records the chronology of the bishops of East Anglia, starting with Felix, 630-647, then going on. Thomas, 647-653; Boniface, 653-669; and Bisus, 669 – 673.

Then the diocese was split into two, with **Dunwich** in the south and **North Elmham,** appropriately enough, in the north. The adjective *north* has faded over the years, as has the *east* in East Dereham.

NORTH ELMHAM	**DUNWICH**
Bedwinnus (673-679)	Etta (673-?)
Northbert	Astwolf
Headulac (around 731)	Eadferth

Edelfrid	Cuthwin
Lanferth	Alberth
Athelwolf (around 811)	Eglaf
Unferth	Herdred
Sibba (around 816)	Alsin
Humferth	Tidferth (787-816)
St Humbert	Weremund
? (killed by Danes 870 or 871)	Wibred

No, this isn't just a list of boring names. They were all of Scandinavian or Nordic origin, maybe Viking, from Viken on the shores of Oslo Fjord, the home of the Vikings. Or maybe from that bit of Schleswig-Holstein north of Hamburg which is called Angeln to this day and was the home of the Angles, hence the English. And, apart from Unferth, they appeared to have a decent lifespan which infers a reasonably settled community and contentment with their religion. It also shows that Dunwich was a *very* important place.

RAILWAYS

THE NORTH NORFOLK COAST has, as you would expect, the **North Norfolk Railway,** better known as the *Poppy Line* and described later, and at Sheringham there are two railway stations, separated by a road. The Poppy Line, rescued from the long-ago M&GN line, runs a single track from its own station from here to Holt, and the other half of the station runs another single line to Norwich where it joins the national network: the name of the franchise holder changes frequently.

There's also the **Wells and Walsingham Light Railway** using a 10¼ track laid on hardcore which once served the M&GNJtR, the *Midland & Great Northern Joint Railway,* familiarly known as the Muddle and Get Nowhere. And there's the trackbed of the *Great Eastern Railway* from King's Lynn to Hunstanton which began life on 3 October 1862 as - would you believe it - the single-track *Lynn & Hunstanton Railway*. No originality!

Before Dr Beeching had his way with the county's rail network, Norfolk was well-endowed. The Great Eastern ran from *Liverpool Street* to *King's Lynn* and *Hunstanton*, with a branch line from *Lynn* to *Swaffham, Dereham, Wymondham* and *Norwich,* and another from *Heacham* to *Wells, Fakenham* and *Dereham*. There was a further loop from *Dereham* to *North Elmham,* and the *East Norfolk*

Railway built the line from *Norwich* to *Cromer*, the bit to *Aylsham* opening on New Year's Day 1880. Two years later the ENR was taken over by the *Great Eastern*, which became part of the *London & North Eastern Railway,* the LNER, in 1923. Back in July 1882 the M&GNJtR linked Aylsham with North Walsham and Melton Constable, but became yet another part of the LNER in 1936, but increasing car traffic killed it in 1952. The last passenger train through Aylsham carried a wreath on the front, saying: "To the memory of another limb of private enterprise which was amputated during the scourge of nationalisation, 1880-1952."

But the Aylsham to Wroxham bit was restored as the privately-run **Bure Valley Railway**; it opened in 1991 and is the county's longest narrow-gauge line.

The Muddle and Get Nowhere ran from *Wisbech North* to *Lynn*, then on to *Fakenham, Melton Constable, Aylsham, Norwich* and *Yarmouth Beach.*

Incorporated in 1845 with £270,000 capital, the *Lynn & Dereham* line was a continuation of the *Lynn & Ely,* and the two soon became the *East Anglian Railway.* The double-track line to Narborough opened on 27 October 1846 and reached Swaffham on 10 August 1847. It struggled on to Sporle by 26 October and entered Dereham on 11 September 1848.

The L&D had major problems: the high cost of land, and cutting through the chalk at Swaffham raised the cost to £24,000 a mile, and bankrupted the contractors. By 1897, completed under new contractors, it was running eight services daily, which rose to nine in 1914 and peaked at twelve in 1955 as a branch of British Railways. From 1900 it took coaches from Doncaster to Yarmouth, and from 1916 added coaches from York. In 1961 the service had collapsed to nine local diesel cars a day; in April 1966 most freight traffic stopped; in August all stations were unmanned, and on 9 September 1968 the line closed. Its revenue was then £22,000 a year, with costs at £46,000. In just thirteen years, how the mighty fell!

The *Norfolk Railway* carved a route from Norwich through Wymondham to Dereham. Authorised in 1845 it hauled freight from 7 December 1846 and passengers from 15 February 1847.

The *Dereham* to *Wells* and *Blakeney* extension got no further than Fakenham, opening on 20 March 1849. The *Wells and Fakenham Railway* finished it, incorporated in 1854; it had cost £10,000 capital from the Earl of Leicester, owner of Holkham Hall;

£14,000 from the town of Wells; and £30,000 from the directors of the Norfolk Railway. The line opened on 1 December 1857, which was declared a local public holiday, with the *Wells Harbour* extension coming in 1859. Although railway engineers in Norfolk benefited from the absence of hard rock, mountains, and wide rivers, the system suffered from a lack of population concentrations and scattered communities.

Then in 1862 the GER absorbed the W&FR, and 30 years later Wells had the luxury of a daily through coach to Liverpool Street. But silting of the harbour reduced goods traffic although day trippers came in their thousands from Norwich, and the line brought many pilgrims to Walsingham.

In decline, the *Wells* to *Heacham* line was a victim of the East Coast floods of January 1953, and the last passenger on the W&FR travelled on 5 October 1964. Freight traffic ceased at the month's end, and by January 1983 the line stopped at North Elmham: this spur closed six years later.

The *Lynn & Fakenham Railway* opened its *Gaywood*-to-*Massingham* track on 16 August 1879, and extended it to Fakenham a year later, to the day, using three locomotives from the Cornish Railway. The M&GN bought the line in 1893 and did reasonable business with farm produce, but passenger traffic was never profitable. The line was at its busiest in the 1930s and carried 571 trainloads of aviation fuel to RAF bases in World War Two. Traffic declined when peace came, and the

Brancaster's AA box is a listed building!

last passenger travelled on 2 March 1959, the last freight on 1 May 1968.

The GER's *Wroxham* to *Dereham* line ran parallel with the M&GN's *Cromer* to *Norwich* line for a mile, near the village of Themelthorpe, after the former went under a bridge carrying the latter. When both lines were facing closure, British Rail abandoned the bridge and joined the lines with the *Themelthorpe Curve*, really a loop, 518 yards of track that opened on 12 September 1960 to accommodate trains laden with concrete beams travelling from Lenwade (A1067, 12 miles NW of Norwich) to sites around the country. When the Ronan Point flats collapsed in East London in 1981 they killed the concrete beam business. The Curve had lost its passenger traffic in 1969 but it closed to goods in January 1982 and the tracks were taken up by 1984. While it was there it looked like a freak of nature on the O.S. map.

The single-track *Lynn & Hunstanton Railway* opened on 3 October 1862, the year that the Prince of Wales bought Sandringham House. Hunstanton had fewer than 500 people in the 1861 census, but had more than 1,000 a decade later as it became fashionable. Snettisham fishermen sent their catch by rail, joining the grain, cattle, manure and coal to form the bulk of the freight traffic.

Hunstanton's L'Estrange family gave most of the ground needed for the line, which was therefore built for less than £60,000. The GER operated the line on an agreement which took half the income, plus £10 per track-mile per week – but the L&HR had to pay compensation when the train hit a bull in August 1863. Seven people were killed as well as the bull.

In 1874 the L&HR merged with the *West Norfolk Junction Railway* and the two were swallowed by the GER on 1 July 1890. The GER doubled the track by 1899, in view of the royal traffic, with the Prince of Wales paying for Wolferton station.

By 1900 there were twelve trains daily each way in summer, six in winter, with connections to Liverpool Street in 187 minutes and to St Pancras in 184. In 1905 a restaurant car was added on golfers' request.

The railways had started a major social revolution in rural Britain, with East Anglia's scattered population benefiting most: never before had so many people been able to afford the luxury of travel. In 1922 there were fourteen summer trains daily, each way, from London to the coast, with extras on Sundays.

Traffic was severely reduced in World War Two, but in the late 1940s summer excursion trains to Hunstanton were packed: nobody minded standing – I know, because I was among them. Just fifteen years later the traffic was on the roads, with homeward vehicles queueing from Sandringham to get through the then bottleneck of King's Lynn. In those days even traffic jams were a novelty – and I know, because I was among them as well.

There was drama on this Hunstanton line in the East Coast floods of 1953. On 31 January the 19.27 down train was caught in the high tide north of Heacham, and a floating bungalow hit the loco's smoke stack, damaged the vacuum brakes, and put the fire out. The train was stuck for six hours with the floodwaters reaching seat level. As the tide receded the footplate crew used the tender floor as fuel and crawled back to Hunstanton. So many beach huts had been washed onto the line that it was blocked until 23 February.

The line was already dying. Diesel cars replaced steam in 1958, and on summer Sundays in 1966 there were just two excursions to Hunstanton from Liverpool Street, and they ceased forever at the season's end.

From 1967 stations were unmanned, and there was only one platform in use at Sunny Hunny (Hunstanton). Level crossing gates in Lynn were replaced by the first automatic barriers in Britain, and all signalling was controlled from Lynn. BR cut the running costs from £100,000 a year to £35,000, but the income of £40,000 also slumped. The line closed on 5 May 1969.

The *West Norfolk Junction Railway* opened the *Heacham* to *Wells* line on 17 August 1866, but the Prince and Princess of Wales had a privilege trip to Holkham on 13 January. The GER operated the line on a partnership, and took it over on 1 July 1890. Its passenger service was an early victim, closing on 2 June 1952. The floods of early 1953 damaged the Burnham Market to Wells section, and forced its closure to passengers: freight traffic to Heacham survived until 28 December 1964.

The *East Norfolk Railway*, incorporated in 1864, began work on the *Whitlingham Junction* (Norwich) to *North Walsham* line in 1865 but stopped when the contractor died and his assets were frozen. Work resumed in 1870 and by 1872 the ENR had Parliamentary approval to extend the track to Cromer - but Cromer didn't want it.

A single track opened to North Walsham on 20 October 1874, to Gunton on 29 July 1876 and, despite the objections, to Cromer on 26 March 1877.

The GER took control in 1881 and between 1896 and 1900, doubled the track to North Walsham. The first train from London took 310 minutes to Cromer, but on 1 July 1897 the daily *Cromer Express* did the journey, non-stop from the big city to North Walsham, in 175 minutes. Renamed the *Norfolk Coast Express* with twelve coaches, this was the pride of the GER until the First World War. After the Second War the *Norfolkman* and the *Broadsman* revived the tradition for a few years.

Then on 18 June 1965 the Post Office chartered the *Orient Express* to come to Cromer to commemorate a new issue of postage stamps. It was the *Orient's* first venture out of Liverpool Street, and the journey was possible only because the only coastal town that didn't want the railway is, with neighbour Sheringham, the only one that still has it. And, for what it's worth, I was on that train as well.

Southgate, King's Lynn

WHAT'S ON THE MENU

NORFOLK HAS SEVERAL culinary masterpieces to call its own. Most of us have heard of the **Norfolk dumpling** if only because it's a nickname for a yokel, a well-endowed son of the soil. The true dumpling, the kind one eats, is simply an unhealthy mixture of plain flour and suet usually with a scattering of currants or sultanas, rolled into balls the size of an apple, and boiled. Refinements are boiling the things in a soup or broth for a bit of flavour, or making a big dumpling, rolling it in a cloth so it looks like the swag that a yokel might have carried on a stick – one dumpling carrying another.

To me – but I'm biased – the most characteristically Norfolk dish is **samphire**. This plant is on sale along the coast in high summer, typically from July to September and is seldom available only a few miles inland. Why? Because it's an edible seaweed that grows in mudflats just below the high tide mark. It's found anywhere on the east coast where the tidal water is calm and devoid of waves, such as in the Humber estuary, The Wash, the coast west of Blakeney Harbour, Breydon Water on the Broads, the River Ore (or Alde) south of Aldeburgh, the Walton backwaters, and the Essex estuaries from the Colne down to Foulness.

It looks something like horsetail, that primitive weed which thrives on poor soil, or like a cluster of miniature sausages impaled on multi-pronged forks. It's a deep green, grows up to nine inches tall, and in September it comes into flower – tiny, bright-yellow things almost too small to see. The largest beds of the stuff, to my knowledge, are on the mudflats near Snettisham.

So what do you do with samphire, which is pronounced *samfur*? As the plant's skeleton is very woody, the only thing to do is steam it for around twenty minutes, grab it by the root, thrust it in the mouth and scrape the flesh off with the teeth. I've seen it on television cook shows, chopped and put in a casserole, and while the diners said "Oooh!" they should have said "Ugh!" because the skeleton is inedible.

Samphire is known in France as St Peter's Plant, *l'herbe de Saint Pierre*, and in botanical circles as glasswort. I love it, but it's an acquired taste which my wife hasn't acquired.

That delicacy of Cromer, the crab, lives on a sea bed which locally is of chalk and sand, and so is clean, and gives the meat its distinctive but subtle sweet flavour.

I haven't acquired a liking for the mobile forms of seafood, such as the mussels which live in the rocks on Hunstanton beach, or the whelks found a few miles out to sea. In that case, do you mind if I don't go into ecstasy by describing them?

NATURE RESERVES

The Norfolk Wildlife Trust at 72 Cathedral Close, Norwich, NR1 4DF, 01603.625540, has 14 reserves. Those in our area, plus the RSPB's two, are:

Roydon Common, 3 miles NE of Lynn on A148 then signposted south. Sandy heath and wetlands, always open.

Narborough Railway Line, 1 mile S of Narborough, SE of Lynn. Disused railway embankment has rich chalk grassland flora & fauna, especially butterflies. Always open.

Snettisham, RSPB, with hides. Common tern, duck. Signed from Snettisham. Always open.

Holme Dunes, north of A149 at Holme. Saltmarsh, dune, wetland. Excellent during migrations with 280 species recorded. Open daily; fee.

Titchwell Marsh, RSPB, with hides; ringed plover, ruff, dunlin, black tern, maybe kingfisher. At low tide, remains of **petrified forest** visible. Shop, WC, picnic site.

Scolt Head Island. See Hunstanton chapter.

Cley Marshes. Major site, more than 300 bird species seen. Hides. Tues-Sun Apr-Oct, 1000-1700.Fee.

Foxley Wood 2 miles N of Bawdeswell, near Themelthorpe Curve site (*see* Railways) Norfolk's largest stand of ancient woodland; butterflies & flowers. Open year round Fri-Wed 1000-1700.

KING'S LYNN
ROYAL NORFOLK
§ indicates things to see

KING'S LYNN HAS BEEN UPGRADED. Before 1537 it was plain old **Bishop's Lynn,** the bishop in question being **Herbert de Losinga** who, in 1094, paid William II some 1,000 marks (£666) for the office and title of Bishop of Norwich.

When Norwich Cathedral was consecrated in 1101, Pope Paschal II learned of the bribe and ordered Bishop de Losinga to built churches and priories as penance. And you thought corruption was modern! Among the buildings was **Holy Mary Magdalene and St Margaret and All Holy Virgins**. Now known as **St Margaret's** it was built on saltmarsh that the bishop owned (so saving him money) in the settlement called Linn, from the Saxon word for a small lake. Linn took the name of Bishop Losinga, later changing it to Bishop's Lynn, with its new §**Saturday** market beside St Margaret's Church.

Bishop Turbe of Norwich (1146-74) was not to be outsmarted by Losinga so he built his own town a mile to the north, gave it the Church of **St Nicholas** and another market, to be held on **Tuesday**. So there were *two* towns – until John granted the Royal Charter in 1204 and so united them. Medieval markets could not survive without royal approval and John allowed both to thrive, which is why Lynn still has two markets to this day. There is also a Friday market, but the large cattle market has gone.

Turbe's town was designed on the grid system with all plots commanding equal rents, as is recorded on a 13th century plan still surviving. When the system was compiled, Turbe's part of town was the more popular so almost all the plots were taken, and the black-robed **Augustinian** friars, reorganised in the 12th century, were lucky to find a site near Tuesday market: their friary is remembered in the name *Austin Street*, where the doorway stands as a sole relic.

The **Dominicans**, known as the *black friars* from their black hoods worn over white cloaks, the **Fransiscans** or *grey friars*, and the **Carmelites**, or *white friars*, all had to find plots in Losinga's Lynn.

§**GREYFRIARS TOWER**, in the beautiful §Tower Gardens near the library, is the only part of the 14th century priory to survive the Dissolution of the Monasteries. A former lantern tower, it was left as a shipmark while the rest of the building was

17

cannibalised, then in 2003 it was featured on BBC Television's *Restoration* programme as it was in a poor state of repair. It never won an award but its needs were far less than many other projects so it stands an excellent chance of surviving at least another century.

An archway of the 12th century **Benedictine** priory stands in *Priory Lane*, south of St Margaret's Church; while *Blackfriars Street* near the museum and *Whitefriars Road* near *Friars Fleet* mark the sites of the other orders.

The Benedictines of St Margaret's Church had rights over the income from the Saturday Market until Bishop John de Grey of Norwich took them over in 1205. The Carmelites – now *they* were weird. They never spoke a word and they slept in their coffins. The Austins were a bit better – they had an altar called the Stairway to Heaven in their church, and they sang Mass over their dead. The Dominicans had a major fire in 1486 when Lynn had more than seventy religious orders, but they – the Grey Friars – escaped the Dissolution of the Monasteries, which is why Greyfriars Tower still stands. The order survived until 1845 – the tower should make it to 2105.

Lynn seemed to have had a love affair with monks. By contrast, Jews were barely tolerated. Many were massacred in 1189 in Jews' Lane, now *Surrey Street* by Tuesday Market, in preparation for Richard I's departure on the Third Crusade. But that expedition was more against the Moslem world than against Jewry. As there were no followers of Islam living in Lynn, it seems that any foreigner was fair game.

FLEET is an old word for 'shallow' – hence 'Fleet' Street marking an old waterway in London. In Lynn the word specifically means 'shallow stream'. The **Millfleet** was bridged in 1250, linking Bishop's Lynn with the village of South Lynn, while the **Purfleet**, the original port, marked the rough boundary between the two Lynns, with **Fisher Fleet** the northern boundary.

The town's location at the mouth of the Great Ouse, sheltered yet prone to flooding, turned the people's minds to maritime trade. From earliest times ships sailed across to the Low Countries and Saxony, bringing back wealth; after the Great Fire of 1331 which destroyed most of the daub-and-wattle-and-thatch houses, the burghers found they could afford to rebuild with brick and tile, brought in by sea. Let the peasants elsewhere in Norfolk stick to mud huts with grass roofs, or use flint if they were lucky!

18

GUILDHALLS

The **Guild of St George**, founded in 1376, met in the 13th century **Hall of the Holy Trinity** where it received its charter from Henry IV in 1406. The hall had escaped the Great Fire but the guildsmen, wanting their own base, built it between 1410 and 1420 by Tuesday Market – and it still stands! It is an unassuming place but as Hitler's War damaged the guildhalls of York and London, St George's is the oldest surviving one in England. Now owned by the National Trust, it is home to a theatre and the King's Lynn Festival.

By contrast, §**TRINITY GUILDHALL** by Saturday Market was completed a year or two later and has a highly distinctive chequerboard appearance from the diligent use of limestone and flint. Yes – it still stands and is one of the most-photographed buildings in Lynn, so shall we give it a miss?

Both guilds stored their wine in the *undercroft* (cellars) and feasted in the main hall. Medieval guilds filled a strange role in society: they were part town council, benevolent society, bank, and trade union, with religious overtones. This was too much for Edward VI so in 1547 he disbanded them and seized most of their assets; after all, Henry VIII had robbed the monasteries and friaries a decade earlier, and it was this move which prompted the name change from Bishop's Lynn to **King's Lynn**. I suppose the act's modern counterpart was the post-war government's fanaticism with nationalisation.

In 1571 the old Trinity undercroft, its timber ceiling replaced by brick barrel-vaulting, became a prison, surviving as such until 1937.

Trinity was restored in the 1950s, the cellars now the §**museum** holding, among other items, the **King John Cup**, the oldest secular loving cup in England, made around 1340 in the reign of Edward III. The **King John Sword** has inscriptions mentioning John and Henry VIII, an unlikely coupling, but is probably Tudor. King John's Charter of 1204 is definitely original, and the Red Register, recording 14th century wills and deeds, is one of the world's oldest paper books.

The museum's exhibits include the Nuremberg Cup of 1634, and a tankard given to Samuel Gurney Creswell in 1853. The locals believe that Samuel, born in Lynn, was the first man to sail the North-West Passage, but history credits Roald Amundsen in 1903-05.

The **Regalia Rooms** are open (not Sunday) Nov-Apr for a fee; access is from the Town Hall next door, built in 1895. The Tourist Office is the old **§ Gaol House**, built in 1784 and in service as the police station until 1935. You may go in the cells. The Jail House is also the place to book a place on a guided walking tour of the town: 01553. 774297.

In Norman times, when the Fens were inundated marshland, the Great Ouse swept in a vast curve a mile wide as it approached Lynn. Straightening began in the 14th century but the present channel was completed in 1853 – and every spadeful removed by hand. **Thoresby College** in Queen Street has a slate marking the site of the quay in 1300. The college, by the way, was founded by the merchant Thomas Thoresby for housing thirteen collegiate priests whose job was to pray, in this life, for his soul in the next life: nice work if you can get it. The college's **§Great Hall** is open to the public and available for private bookings on 01255.766922. The place is now run by the King's Lynn Preservation Trust.

REBUILDING THE TOWN

The town was gradually rebuilt a second time (the first time was after the fire of 1331) between 1550 and 1650 in clay brick, fired in kilns in Gaywood and West Lynn. The Corporation bought the bricks at £5 per thousand in 1613, yet in 1437 it had bought 200,000 bricks for the South Gate for £50 – and in the 1930s Fletton bricks were selling for £1.10/- (£1.50) a thousand. But *they* were mass-produced. Thatch was forbidden, so roofing tiles were shipped in from the Netherlands; no problem for a maritime town.

The **Hanseatic Warehouse** was built in the 1480s, in brick, by German merchants, on land given by Edward IV. **Marriott's Barn**, also near the river, has stone walls to withstand floods, its timber superstructure probably being 16th century German work. The warehouse was renamed **St Margaret's House** after Edward Everard bought it in 1751 for St Margaret's Church. The Hanseatic League? It was a north-German medieval protection society for merchants, which collapsed in England during the Thirty Years' War of 1618-48, but which survived in Germany. Hamburg is still known as a *Hansestadt*, a Hanseatic town. Mr Everard? It's a well-known name in the town.

20

§ CUSTOMS HOUSE

One of the classic buildings of Lynn is the Customs House on the Purfleet, financed by Charles Turner of Warham but built in 1683 by local man Henry Bell, son of a local merchant and responsible for the design of North Runcton church; look on the south wall of the House for the sculpted heads wearing corn ears and grapes. Upstairs is the Long Room, where ships' masters 'made their report' on the voyage just completed, and importers 'made entry' into the records. Regardless of length, all such places were called long rooms after the original in the London Customs House. This building was one of many featured in the box-office flop *Revolution*, filmed in the town. The Purfleet has been cleared of rotting hulls in recent years and cleaned up with a statue of Captain Vancouver now keeping guard.

North of Purfleet is Ferry Lane which leads to the passenger ferry operating to West Lynn for a small fee.

Captain Vancouver

CAPTAIN VANCOUVER

LYNN'S ELEVENTH- CENTURY seagoing merchants shipped out wool, fish and salt, and returned with millstones, limestone and timber for building, and furs. A century later, Brughes and Ghent had joined the trade which was concentrating on wool and cloth as exports as East Anglia prospered. The abbeys of Ely and Peterborough sent out vast quantities of wool – in 1267 Lynn handled 1406 sacks of it worth £3,440. The previous year Lynn imported wine from Gascony, including 50 tuns (12,600 gallons) for Henry II.

Lynn saw commerce as its main income and

soon it was importing exotics such as Russian beeswax, Finnish timber, Icelandic fish – and pilgrims for Walsingham. By 1604 Lynn was almost as busy as Bristol, with 96 shiploads in and 159 out.

Of course, smuggling was an inevitable sideline, a typical incident being the discovery in 1718 of a load of brandy in a man's home. The poor sod was whipped around the town.

But what of Captain Vancouver? Patience! A few years after the whipping incident Lynn was sending five whalers each May to Greenland, returning in July with their catches, and eventually in 1605 the trade built the **§Greenland Fishery** in Bridge Street. Other trade took in lead from Dorset, furs from Norway, dyes from Picardy, and sent out corn to Scotland, cloth to Denmark and wool to Italy.

It was the perfect background for **George Vancouver**. He was born in 1757 on New Conduit Street, the son of the deputy Collector of Customs at Purfleet.

Vancouver had every encouragement to embark on a seagoing career. In 1771 he joined Captain Cook on the *Resolution* for a four-year voyage around the world. In 1776 he signed on as midshipman on Cook's last voyage, aboard *Discovery*. And what did they discover? A mid-Pacific archipelago which they named the Sandwich Islands in honour of John Montagu Sandwich, First Lord of the Admiralty, the man who liked eating snacks when he played cards. George Vancouver was among the sailors who retrieved Cook's body after the islanders murdered him and, much later, the islands were renamed Hawaii.

Vancouver was back in the isles in 1791-92, persuading the Sandwichians to become part of the British Empire (which is why the Union Jack is in the Hawaiian flag, the only American state to carry it). Vancouver also took Western Australia whose inhabitants could not object.

Then George sailed to Canada, negotiating for the Spanish to cede to Britain (England and Scotland had had a wedding ceremony in 1707) territories from the Alaska Panhandle to the Great Lakes. Some of the territory became British Columbia, whose largest city is now called Vancouver – but the man from whom it is named died at Petersham, Surrey, aged just forty. In recent years a statue of him has been put up in Purfleet, near the Customs House, and a shopping centre bears his name.

WALLS AND GATES

BISHOP'S LYNN had been well-defended since its beginning. At the south, by **Friar's Fleet,** (known as the *River Nar* by outsiders, the *Esk* by townspeople, and the *Puny River* by people from Middleton village); on the west by the Great Ouse; on the north by Purfleet and Fisherfleet. That left only the landward approach from the east.

In 1294 Edward I gave Lynn the right to levy *murage*, a tax on inward goods to raise money for building the town wall – *mur* is 'wall' in French. The wall was just an earth embankment, but the gates, and nearby fortifications protecting Turbe's town, were of stone. East Gate, demolished in 1800, stood on today's Littleport Street, and Dowshill Gate was near Alexandra Dock.

Two gates survive. **North Guanock Gate** to the east has been much restored, but **§SOUTH GATE** is the most impressive medieval gateway in East Anglia (others are in Castle Acre and Norwich), as traffic still surges through it.

The present gate was built in 1437 of brick faced with stone, probably on the site of the first gate of Edward II's reign and one of the first times that brick was used in the town. Maintenance for that original wall fell on villagers as far as Castle Acre and Stoke Ferry, but the people of Lynn were responsible for the later gate. Robert Hertanger, a London mason, was paid £100 up front to build it but proved himself to be one of the early cowboy builders because he drank the money instead and was sacked. The corporation had to hire another mason.

None of Lynn's defences was tested in battle, but South Gate was threatened during the *Civil War* of 1642-49 when Royalists under Sir Hamon L'Estrange (you'll meet this name again in Hunstanton) seized the town and were besieged by Parliamentarians led by the Earl of Manchester. After Lynn's water supply was cut off, the gate surrendered.

In the Middle Ages the gatekeeper charged tolls on goods entering town, closed the gate at dusk and, when bubonic plague was around, kept out all visitors who couldn't prove a need to enter. Robert Anthony, appointed keeper in 1509, was also 'cleanser of the muckhills' as the town's rubbish was dumped outside South Gate and, as this muck included Robert's own faeces (from the 'privy' on the gate's upper floor), he certainly got his own back.

Later gatekeepers took a percentage of the tolls, but on 25 March 1723 the last keeper was dismissed as tolls were abolished on that day. The gates themselves remained until 1795. The council still appoints a gatekeeper whose only task is to open the building to the public, *Wednesdays*, June-Sep, 1.30 to 4.30, for a small fee.

§**Red Mount Chapel** was never part of the defences although it's nearby. Built around 1485 by friars, it supplied lodging to pilgrims who had sailed into Lynn and were going to walk to Walsingham. After the dissolution of the friaries in 1538 and the collapse of the Walsingham pilgrimage, Red Mount Chapel lost its customers, yet it has survived as an octagonal building on its own small mound. For years Lynn had an **honest lawyer**; it was the name of a pub close to the gates, but it is now a guest house.

WITCHES AND CHURCHES

Margaret Read was burning at the stake in Tuesday Market in 1590 when her heart burst from her body and flew across the market square. You want proof? Then look for a diamond-shaped brick high in a wall in the north-east corner of the square showing where poor Maggie's heart struck. Legend claims it then bounced down Water Lane and into the river, but I think that's stretching it a bit far.

Normally the crime of sorcery was punished by hanging, but if a witch had, allegedly, used her powers to kill anybody, then the penalty quite often was death by fire. Elizabeth Housegoe died that way in 1598, as did Mary Smith in 1616. Mary had supposedly bewitched Elizabeth Hancocke who died after Mary called "a pox to light on you." A prosecution witness was the Reverend Mr Roberts who, in 1615, had laid a water main to the house that Maggie Read's heart struck.

And in 1646 Lynn Corporation paid £5 to Matthew Hopkins, the **Witchfinder General**, for finding two witches in the town and seeing them hang in Tuesday Market. Hopkins, born in Ipswich and practising as a solicitor in Manningtree, was a right bad 'un who killed more poor misguided and misunderstood women than any other person in the country.

Maybe it's not fair to talk of witches and churches together, but if there is a link it must surely be **Hallowe'en**. Lynn's oldest surviving church, **All Saints'**, was known to its Saxon founders as *All Hallows*, but not in modern English, of course. You know that

24

November 1st is All Saints' Day in the Christian calendar, a public holiday in most of Europe but we don't even get a day off.

The present **All Saints'** church was rebuilt in the 14th century, with little added since. Its main interest is the *anchorhold*, a cell in which hermits volunteered to be locked for the remainder of their days. Records show that the anchorhold was occupied in 1272, 1477, and the 16th century, the inmate's needs being satisfied by a servant living next door. It's still there: ring 01553.763044 to see it.

The mother church is §**St Margaret's**, founded in 1101 by Herbert de Losinga, but little of the original remains. In the 12th century two towers were added at the west end, to be heightened in the 14th century. Soon the north-west tower began leaning as it was on poor soil: in 1453 the clergy built a larger tower around it for support. Despite this problem, in the 16th century the other tower had a 258ft spire added.

And then came the storm of 8 September 1741 which demolished steeple and tower, hurling the masonry onto the roof. George II and Sir Robert Walpole, MP for Lynn, each gave £1,000 and the borough raised £3,000 by taxation. The tower was replaced, but not the steeple.

The nave has several treasures: the richly-decorated **pulpit** was probably made by Matthew Brettingham, the man who built the main staircase at Holkham Hall. He included the Hebrew letters of the *Tetragrammaton*, the name of the 'Unmentionable One', Jehovah or Yahwe, sometimes spelled as JHVH or even YHWH. Look for the mayor's official pew; also for the reredos (ornamental screen) showing Felix, a preacher who was befriended by badgers after being shipwrecked at **Babingley**, a hamlet near Sandringham. Felix became the first Bishop of Dunwich, and Felixstowe is named from him. The side chapel is said to have England's largest brass memorial, this to Adam de Walsoken who died in 1349. And Walsoken is a village stuck on the backside of Wisbech. I should know: I was born there.

Lynn has always been subject to high-tide flooding so the clock on **St Margaret's** south tower shows the tides, the 1 to 12 being replaced by letters spelling LYNNHIGHTIDE. It was installed in 1603 but recent floods have worsened, as is shown by tidemarks. In ascending order they read March 1961, March 1949, March 1883, Jan 1953 (the East Coast Floods) and Jan 1978. Some people say the sea is rising; it's a fact that the land here is sinking.

St Nicholas's Chapel, the town's third church, was built in the 13th and 15th centuries and is now used only for concerts in the King's Lynn Festival. It suffers from severe subsidence.

LYNN MISCELLANY

Numbers 28, 30, and 32 in **King Street** are on the site of a medieval stone hall. At the Market Lane junction with Chapel Street is **Lattice House**, once a block of shops and homes in a long building and later one of the town's then 400 inns, a reminder that until modern times the water supply was undrinkable.. **Clifton House** in Queen Street, distinguished by the spiralled columns by the front door, was built in the 16th century on a crypt of the 14th.

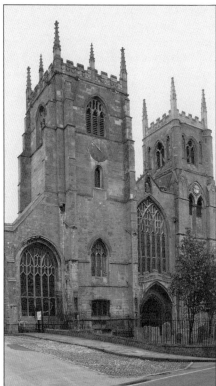

St Margaret's Church, King's Lynn

Lynn was one the hundred-odd English **rotten boroughs,** granted the right in 1558 to have its own Member of Parliament – but Lynn had *two* members. At one time both seats were under the patronage of Thomas Howard, fourth Duke of Norfolk, and were available only to the landed gentry. In 1675 Robert Coke of Holkham spent £10,000 on his election, and later MPs included Lord George Bentinck, leader of the Protectionist Party, and Lord Stanley, son of the Earl of Derby. The Derby in question is a hamlet on the south-east tip of the Isle of Man, where a certain horse race was founded

Not many tourist attractions are in industrial estates, but **Caithness Glass** is an exception. You will find the visitor centre on the large Hardwick Road Estate, offering tours of the glassblowing works and selling examples of intricate glassware. The firm closed a few years ago but is now open as part of the Edinburgh Crystal Glass Company. There are sister shops in Perth and Edinburgh.

BEYOND THE TOWN
§CASTLE RISING

CASTLE RISING is both a castle and a village. Before 1066, 'Rysyng' was owned by Stigand, the Lord of the Manor of Snettisham, the man who crowned Harold in 1066 on his way south to the Battle of Hastings. The modern village is small, rebuilt in the 12th century to make way for the castle, which was begun around 1138 by **William d'Albini**, whose family came from Normandy but presumably hitched their allegiance to this new island-nation, as *Albini* is a corruption of Albion – England. Much of the earthwork was done later, proved by the discovery of the buried half of a silver penny minted between 1158 and '80: it had been cut to make two half-pennies.

D'Albini was also Lord of the Manors of Buckenham and Happisburgh, and he married Maud Bigod, of the family which was soon to produce the dukedom of Norfolk. D'Albini built the priory at Wymondham where, in 1833, workmen found what is believed to be Maud's lead-lined coffin.

You're in the mood for a little family diversion? Here goes. Maud died in childbirth but their surviving son, **William II**, married the widow of Henry I and so gained **Arundel Castle** in Sussex. A daughter of a much later Earl of Arundel married into the Howard Dukes of Norfolk, which resulted in the Norfolks moving their family seat to Arundel, where they still are.

The D'Albinis continued to hold the earldom of Sussex and the manors of Arundel, Buckenham, and Rising, later adding the vast estates of the Clare family of **Clare**, Suffolk. And *they* owned County Clare in Ireland! The fourth William d'Albini was with King John at the signing of *Magna Carta*, but he died in 1221 on the way home from the Fifth Crusade. By the mid-13th century Rising Castle needed major repairs, which were probably done by Robert Montalt, Lord of Rising from 1299 to 1329. He sold the castle for 10,000 marks (£6,666) in 1327 to Edward III, who'd just acceded to the throne, and Montalt's widow sold her remaining rights to Queen Isabella in 1331. *Phew!*

Edward II was murdered in September 1327, allegedly by having a red-hot poked pushed up his anus. His widow, also Isabella, was imprisoned in Rising on suspicion of being involved in the ghastly act. She went mad, and her screams are said to haunt the castle to this day, a truly ghostly act.

Castle Rising eventually passed to the **Black Prince**, the son of Edward III, who died in 1376, the year before he would have become king, but he had decreed that Rising be held in perpetuity by the Duchy of Cornwall. In fact it stayed duchy property only until 1544 when Henry VIII gave the castle and the manor to **Thomas Howard, third Duke of Norfolk,** and his son Henry, Earl of Surrey. So it is the Howard family who has held the place in perpetuity.

King Henry beheaded Earl Henry in January 1547 and threatened father, the duke, with an identical fate on the 28th of that month. But early that day the king it was who died, and the duke was spared. The tombs of Thomas, Henry, and the Arundel daughter, are all in §**Framlingham** Church in Suffolk and you will never regret going there to see them.

THE CASTLE TODAY.

Castle Rising stayed with the Howards until 1958 when English Heritage became involved. Only the keep and the gatehouse survive, but the keep is large and in good condition, as befits its other name of *donjon*, meaning 'power' The massive earthworks which surrounded the castle are intact, enclosing around twelve acres, but little remains of the curtain wall that stood on top.

The keep has similarities with that of Norwich Castle, and both may have been copies of the castle at Falaise, Normandy. The keep is 78.5 ft long, plus 20 ft for the forebuilding which guards the main door, by 68.5 ft wide, with walls rising to 50 ft.

The steps to the main door at first-floor level are impressive, but the great hall, at the same level, lost its grandeur when it lost its roof and floor.

RISING VILLAGE

The village church, which has its tower at the transept crossing, has plaques to several members of the Howard family which produced numerous Dukes of Norfolk, and the present Lord Howard of Rising has been the owner since 1978 although English Heritage maintains the place, and EH members have free entry.

There are ruins of the Norman church of Rising, abandoned when the village was moved, and rediscovered in the 19th century.

Rising village was another of those **rotten boroughs**, with two MPs from 1558 to 1832, one of them being Sir Robert Peel of Houghton Hall, ten miles away, and our first *Prime Minister*.

There is a little ditty:

Rising was a sea-port town when Lynn was but a marsh.
Now Lynn it is a sea-port town and Rising fares the worse.

The rhyme gives you some idea of the Norfolk pronunciation for 'worse'.

The old road to Hunstanton, before the bypass, ran through the village, with a nasty bend at **Onion Corner**, named from the crop which was seemingly grown every year here and made quite a stink.

THE SANDRINGHAM ESTATE

ALBERT-EDWARD, Prince of Wales, was house-hunting. His parents, Queen Victoria and Prince Albert, wanted him to have a country home when he was twenty-one. On 4 February 1862, Prince A-Edward saw **Sandringham Hall** and asked his mother to buy it: the price was only £220,000.

The prince extended the hall and in March 1863 brought his bride here, Princess Alexandra of Denmark. Further extensions were needed, then the prince demolished the main part and built anew.

In November 1891 fire damaged fourteen upper-storey rooms, but the prince went ahead with plans to add more bedrooms to hold his fiftieth birthday party here The repairs inevitably gave him the opportunity to add yet more bedrooms.

The prince's son, who became *George* V, brought his own bride to a small house in the grounds and later renamed it **York Cottage.** As their family grew, so the cottage was extended, and it was here that *George VI* was born.

The Royal Family tends to use Sandringham House as a winter retreat, and it was from here that George V made his first Christmas Day radio broadcast in 1932, with Queen Elizabeth II giving her first televised Christmas message from here in 1957.There were further extensions to the property between 1973 and '76, and in 1977 the Queen decided to open the §house and grounds to the public.

Sandringham House
By gracious permission of HM The Queen

THE ESTATE

The estate covers 20,600 acres, 32 square miles, and includes the villages of Anmer, Babingley, Flitcham, Great Bircham, Shernborne, West Newton, Wolferton, and parts of Dersingham, with 600 of those acres open free to the public as a country park with marked walks. Sandringham is not classed as a village, although it has a church; Domesday recorded it as *Sant Dersingham.*

The estate is the Monarch's personal property and is run commercially, its profits helping to maintain the house. Much of the land is worked by tenant farmers, but the Queen also farms, has forestry, and a stud farm. There's also the fruit farm at Appleton, popular for pick-your-own.

§SANDRINGHAM HOUSE

ESTATE AGENT'S HYPOTHETICAL ADVERT:

Elegant Country House. XXX bedrooms, YYY reception rooms, ZZZ* kitchens, elaborate staff quarters. This smart home with major extensions commands splendid views over fields and farms and includes numerous specialist rooms, notably a two-storey main drawing room, elegant dining room, sumptuous ballroom.

Currently owned by prestigious family with holiday homes in central London, Windsor, and Scotland.

Offered with 90 acres of mature gardens in which are set several outbuildings known as the Sandringham Museum and consisting of coach house, fire station and power house currently housing a collection of automobiles possibly second only to that at Beaulieu, Hants, and including a 1900 Tonneau (first car bought by owning family), saloon of 1913, brougham of 1928, and shooting-brake of 1937, all built by Messrs Daimler.

Prospective buyers need access to Fort Knox, USA. Outgoings: extortionate. Asking price: inestimable.

Offers not accepted.

To view: join queue at main gate where inspection times and dates are shown. Prospective buyers' warning: hundreds of strangers may be found on the premises on specified days.

If you can't get in, look for the elegant wrought-iron §**Norwich Gates** made for the Great Exhibition of 1862, later a wedding gift for the Prince and Princess of Wales.

Number of rooms is a Crown secret!

THE VILLAGES

The first village after Castle Rising is tiny **Babingley,** whose sign shows **St Felix** in his ship. Legend claims that Felix built the first church in East Anglia here, around 630, to be followed much later by

Continued on page 34

BIRCHAM MILL

Great Bircham village is 4 miles north of the A148 at Harpley and 6 miles east of the A149 at Dersingham, and Bircham Mill lies on the western side of the village. It has been lovingly restored to full working order and visitors can climb to the top of the building and out on the fan staging. The machinery is in place and the sails turn on windy days. Adjoining is the original bakery where a range of bread is still baked, except Saturdays, for visitors to buy. Wholemeal and white bread, rolls, scones, teacakes and sponge cakes are just some of the goodies available.

Our tearooms serve a full range from decaffeinated cappuccinos to camomile tea, and traditional tea served generously by the pot. Cream teas are our speciality but we also serve dairy-free tea bread, flapjacks, shortbread, Cornish pasties, filled rolls, soup and baked potatoes plus much more; naturally, all our bread and cakes are hand-made on site.

Bircham Mill is the ideal place to relax in the garden and let the children play in the under-7s area; slightly older children can tackle our free treasure hunt or test their countryside knowledge in our stable-room quizzes.

Why not try our cycle hire? There are miles of quiet roads for cyclists of all ages and abilities to explore. We have child seats, tag-alongs and burley trailers, tandems and individual bikes from very small to very tall. Routes, helmets and back-up are provided, free of charge.

Humphrey Cottage is self-catering and adjoins the mill, and is available Easter to October. It offers the perfect escape, with wonderful walking and cycling on the doorstep and the King's Head pub a short walk away. Beaches and birdwatching are just a 10-minute drive away.

Bircham Mill

HOUGHTON HALL

HOUGHTON HALL

Houghton Hall, 13 miles east of King's Lynn, 10 miles west of Fakenham and near the A148, is one of the finest examples of Palladian architecture in England. Built in the 1720s for Sir Robert Walpole, Britain's first Prime Minister, the original designs were by James Gibbs and Colen Campbell, with interior decoration by William Kent. The Marquess of Cholmondeley has restored the house to its former grandeur, with magnificently furnished staterooms containing many of their original furnishings, enabling the visitor to step back in time and enjoy Houghton as it may have been in Walpole's day.

The Hall is set in 350 acres of parkland, home to a large herd of white fallow deer. The 5-acre walled garden has been divided, by clipped and sculptured yew hedges and some statues, into areas devoted to fruit and vegetables, herbaceous borders, croquet lawn, formal rose garden with more than 150 varieties, and glasshouses. The design of the rose garden is based on the ceiling of the White Drawing Room in the Hall, with statues and a sunken fountain. Julian and Isabel Bannerman designed the rustic temple and the octagonal fruit cage, which is a feature of the kitchen garden. The main garden is full of colour all summer.

The unique Model Soldier Collection, one of the largest and most comprehensive in the world, contains more than 20,000 models arranged in various battle formations from Waterloo to the Western Desert. The licensed restaurant provides waitress-serviced lunches and teas; there is a well-stocked shop, and picnic and children's play area. For details of opening times phone: 01485.528569.

a stone church abandoned in 1861. The present church of corrugated iron and thatch was the gift of Edward VII.

The countryside here is very sandy, supporting conifers, heathers and rhododendrons, where grass snakes and deer can be found. It is a truly beautiful landscape especially in May and June.

The second turning on the left, as you go north, a loop road leads to **Wolferton,** noted for its §**railway station** §**church,** and §**village sign**, one of many in the county. The wolf in the sign is the legendary **Fenrir**, an evil beast who terrorised the villagers. The Norse god Woden, from whom Wednesday is named, sent the villagers a cord with which to restrain Fenrir – but he would wear it only if a man put his hand in the beast's mouth. Tyr volunteered for the job and by the time Fenrir realised he was harnessed, Tyr should have been renamed the one-armed.

Wolferton's Church of St Peter, built in carrstone around 1310 near where Felix came ashore, has several oddities. There are 13th century stone coffins by the door, and a stone seat recalling the days before pews when the old and infirm leaned against the wall. Outside the south side of the chancel there is a small window seat set low to allow lepers to follow the service without contaminating other people.

The railway runs no more. The elegant station was converted to a museum of railway and regal memorabilia, but it is now two separate and elegant homes, one on the *up* platform, the other on the *down*.

Many of the Sandringham Estate staff live at **West Newton**, which is distinctive for its large water tower, built for Appleton Farms in 1877, with homes for two families beneath the tank: they would certainly live with a weight on their shoulders. When Appleton Hall was burned out in 1707, the Paston family, famed for the Paston Letters (of which more later, at the end of the book) quit, and the Church of St Mary was abandoned. Its round tower is more likely Norman than Saxon.

Flitcham was originally Felixtown, another reminder of Bishop Felix. Abbey Farm is on the site of an Augustinian Priory built around 1251. The only thing I've found to say about tiny **Anmer** is that it has one of the steepest hills in Norfolk, around one in ten. **Shernborne's** church is on the site of East Anglia's second-oldest chapel – another relic of Felix's presence. The modern church was rebuilt by the Prince of Wales who became Edward VII, and the village sign shows Sir Thomas de Shernborne, who became Chamberlain to Henry VI's queen, Margaret of Anjou. But it was all such a long time ago.

The sea is now $2^1/_2$ miles away, but **Dersingham** was a fishing port in medieval times, and Henry VI granted its fishermen the freedom of the seas: that's before we heard of the Common Fisheries Policy, of course. On land, there were seven manors after the Norman Conquest, for the tide has turned for the Royal Estate now owns much of Dersingham. St Nicholas's Church's first recorded vicar came in 1106; there's a 12th century coffin lid inside the door, and there's also a wooden chest almost seven feet long which was made before 1360. Yet the church itself is pure 14th-century, with a 15th-century hammerbeam roof. Dersingham churchyard holds the Great Barn, bearing the date 1671 July 13, and the county council maintains it. It really was all such a long time ago – and that's the charm of this part of the country: it's undisturbed, unspoiled, undeveloped.

But there *are* modern attractions. **Dersingham Pottery** in Chapel Road throws porcelain and stoneware and is open to view most days; and **High Farm** has Suffolk Punch and similar breeds of heavy horse still working the land. Come for a demonstration and a ride on a hay wain, Easter to September.

BEYOND THE ROYAL ESTATE

Great Bircham has been home to humanity since the Bronze Age, as is shown by burial mounds on the common, which have yielded bones and jewellery. Much more modern graves are also here, in the War Graves Cemetery by the Church of St Mary the Virgin. George VI unveiled the cross here in 1946 showing where 66 Allied and eleven German aircrew lie, plus one servicewoman. The church still has its box pews, and above the Norman arch are the heraldic arms of George III. Undisturbed, unspoiled, undeveloped.

But the main attraction in the village is §**BIRCHAM MILL**, the only working windmill in this part of the county. See page 32 for the story and picture.

By contrast, **BIRCHAM NEWTON** is much-restored and has long been in the forefront of events. The **Royal Flying Corps** came here in 1916 and their base was rebuilt in 1929 and was soon to become a major World War Two airfield, where **617 Squadron**, the

35

Dam Busters, trained with Barnes Wallis's bouncing bomb. The RAF moved out in 1960 and seven years later the base became the **Bircham Newton Training Centre** which began teaching building crafts, notably how to build brick walls. The trouble is, somebody has to knock them down again.

Not only is the village itself tiny, but its church is one of the smallest in the county. There are no porches, no windows on the north and just four on the south, while the east one is small. The floor is brick, and the Victorian box pews are still in place. The church would make a good setting for a film on Dickensian poverty – yet it wasn't poor. And Nelson's daughter Horatia married Philip Ward, the local rector, and raised a large family at Church Farm.

OTHER VILLAGES, SMALL, SMALL &SMALLER

Nearby is **Bircham Tofts**, which Domesday recorded as *Stofstan,* referring to its stony soil although the linguisics are now lost. The parish merged with Bircham Newton in 1719 but the church remained in use until 1941. East of Lynn along the B 1145 is **Leziate**, a hamlet amid beautiful heatherstrewn countryside; even the sand-pits are full of life, from martins to lizards. **Gayton** has little to offer as its windmill is derelict, but its name contrasts with that of **Grimston**, suggesting it may be the 'devil's town'. The church at **East Walton** has some box pews but the priory ruins are on private land and so inaccessible. The B 1145 leads on to **Great Massingham**, whose church has an enormous tower. St Andrew's in **Little Massingham** was founded by the Saxons, indicating that it is younger than its greater namesake, but the church's oldest part is a solitary Norman window. Sir John L'Estrange – see next chapter – was buried here in 1517 because of a clause in his will beginning *if I die within five miles of Massingham...* **Harpley** sits south of the A 148, its Church of St Lawrence rebuilt by Sir Robert Knollys, who pronounced it Knowles, commander of the English troops in the wars with France under Edward III and Richard II. Its interior is big, bare, and forbidding, and the 15th century pews and 14th century rood are still in place. And now for something much bigger.

§HOUGHTON HALL – background

In 1715 Sir Robert Walpole became First Lord of the Treasury and Chancellor of the Exchequer. This made him prime among government ministers, and so he became England's first Prime Minister, a post he held for 22 years, helped now and then by his brother-in-law 'Turnip' Townshend (see Holkham Hall).

Robert was the fifth of nineteen children – pity their poor mother! – born on the Houghton estate in 1676. He went to a private school in Great Massingham, then on to Eton and Cambridge; while he was there, sampling the ale-houses, his two older brothers died, leaving him heir to the estate. At 24 he married the daughter of the Lord Mayor of London, and claimed his inheritance in 1710 on his father's death. And he was only 35.

He followed family tradition by entering Parliament, as he *owned* the Castle Rising seat. He was, of course, a Whig. Moving on to the seat for King's Lynn, which he also owned, Walpole rose quickly through the ranks: Secretary at War, Treasurer of the Navy. But in 1712 he was in the Tower of London, convicted of bribery involving a mere £2,000. In later life he claimed that bribery and corruption were essential elements in the business of statesmanship, and that every man had his price. (So what's new?)

In 1714 Queen Anne was dying and the ruling Tories were negotiating the succession of James Edward, a Catholic. Walpole and other leading Whigs burst into the Royal bedchamber and persuaded Anne to let them take over the administration. This bold strategy gave not only a new government but a new monarch, as James Edward gave way to the Whigs' nominee, George I. True, he spoke only German, but he *was* a Protestant.

Walpole saved the nation from bankruptcy after the South Sea Bubble (in modern terms this was a Stock Market fix in which shares in a trading company were hyped out of all proportion, then crashed), but found himself obliged to give the new king, George II, £100,000 a year from the Civil List. A grateful king gave Walpole his town house at **10, Downing Street,** but Walpole accepted it not as a personal gift but as the official residence of the First Lord of the Treasury, which is still is. Walpole resigned in 1742, became the First Earl of Orford (Suffolk) with an annual pension of £4,000, and devoted his remaining years to his dream home in north Norfolk, Houghton Hall. He died on 18 March 1745, leaving the Houghton estate deep in debt.

Probably the most surprising treasure is the Royal Throne which is seen on television every year at the State Opening of Parliament, and spends the rest of its time here.

SOME NORTH NORFOLK BIRDS

Avocet

Redshank

Kestrel

Marsh Harrier

Lapwing (Peewit)

Dunlin

NOT TO SCALE

Curlew

Oystercatcher

Shelduck

Great Crested Grebe (summer)

Ringed Plover

38

HUNSTANTON
ROMAN NORFOLK

HUNSTANTON IS UNIQUE. It has the only red and white §cliffs in England and it is the only east coast resort to face west. Hunstanton faces the setting sun and, when the tide is low in The Wash, you can see glimpses of the coast of Lincolnshire, including 'the Stump', the 272ft 6in tower of St Botolph's Church at Boston. Boston is said to take its name from Botolph and, of course, it lent the name to Massachusetts.

But back to Hunstanton. The resort began in Victorian times and depended heavily on the railway. Edward, Prince of Wales, came here to recover from a severe attack of typhoid and so publicised the town.

RESORT RÉSUMÉ. And what does the town have? An excellent beach, with a few creeks in it at low water and, north of the pier, a good scattering of carrstone rocks on that beach, covered with weed and beds of mussels and making it ideal for children. It has the stump of a once-elegant pier, a large and pleasant green on the slope from town centre to beach, a lighthouse, and several amusements for the crowds. It is a resort that appeals to children and the young, to families, and it has a good sprinkling of retirement homes. It does *not* have a railway, nor industry of any size. You can see the town in half a day, but there's plenty to keep families engaged all week.

Sunny Hunny lost its pier in 1978 but it has added numerous attractions. Foremost is §**HUNSTANTON SEA LIFE SANCTUARY** on South Promenade, which has the SEAL HOSPITAL attached. Formerly known as The Kingdom of the Sea, it is a twin to the attraction at the other end of the county, in Great Yarmouth, though the head office is in Poole, Dorset. It is open daily except Christmas. Phone 01485.533576. Seals and penguins are each fed three times daily, and otters twice. Sharks just have one meal, at 1.30. The attraction began as a refuge for injured or lost seals and seal pups, but the other aquatic creatures were never brought in as waifs.

The nearby **OASIS** is billed as an all-weather seafront leisure centre and is run by West Norfolk District Council offering indoor and outdoor pools, squash, aerobics, and a fitness suite. 01485.534227.

And you can cruise to **Seal Island**, which is a sandbank out in The Wash and home to grey and common seals. This is run by Searles (01485.534211), a local firm big in holiday entertainment, which sails from the central promenade, often in amphibian craft. The wartime **DUKW** (pronounced 'duck') still operates so long after the Normandy landings and is a floating museum-piece. Elsewhere you have bingo, nine-hole golf, and a glorious beach.

In short, it's a *pleasant* town; even shorter, it's *two* towns – **Old Hunstanton** to the north and **St Edmund's** to the south, named from its church, built in 1865. Old Hunstanton was the home of the Le Strange (L'Estrange or le Strange: I've seen these variations) family for nine centuries, and their hall was a moated mansion which has suffered severely in two fires, in 1853 and more recently. Sir Henry Le Strange's brass in **St Mary's** church marks his death in 1506, and there are records which tell that in 1286 Nicholas Bragge was beheaded on his second conviction for theft, the only known instance of this punishment for this

Hunstanton lighthouse

crime in England. When I was here as a child there was the rumour that the L'Estranges still owned the beach, and there was certainly a wreck rotting away on its sands.

Currently the family name is remembered in the Old Barns Antiques and Crafts Centre, billed as 'the finest combined collection'

40

of these items in Norfolk. The exhibits frequently change but currently include teddy bear and clock making, wooden toys and painted glass, and waterpaintings mainly of the locality.

Bishop Aelfric of Elmham, who's not in that list on page 9, gave land at 'Hunstanes tune' (town) to St Edmund's Abbey at Bury. The abbot built St Edmund's Chapel in Old Hunston (a local variation on the name) to mark the spot where the saint reputedly came ashore; today the ruins (open daily) are near the lighthouse, which is *not* working. So did the saint climb the cliff, or was his boat washed up on a giant wave? Or maybe parachutes are older than we think. The saint is also shown in a window in his new church in the *new* town.

HEACHAM

WHO WOULD HAVE DREAMED of meeting a native American (in pre-PC days called a Red Indian) in Heacham? Maybe not the real person, but in the Church of St Mary the Virgin there's a monument to §**Princess Pocatontas**.

Let us begin with the **Rolfe** family who were to Heacham what the l'Estranges were to Hunstanton. John Rolfe, born in 1585, sailed to Virginia in 1609, losing his wife and baby in a shipwreck. He went alone to Jamestown, the first English colony in America and founded just two years earlier, and there he fell in love with 14-year-old Pocahontas.

But let us go back further. Captain John Smith (who had worked at Lynn) was one of the builders of Jamestown. When he had gone exploring this new continent he was captured by native Americans and taken to their chief, Powhatan (say *pow-hát-an*), who ordered him to be killed. Powhatan's daughter, Pocahontas, then around twelve, threw herself at Smith and so saved his life. She thus became the link between the natives and the Europeans, and was the first Amerind to be baptised.

Let's go forward to Rolfe. He and Pocahontas married, and grew tobacco in Jamestown. Their son Thomas was born in 1615 and the next year the family sailed for England. They certainly came to Heacham, and legend claims they planted a mulberry tree at Heacham Hall. They went on to London where Pocahontas was presented to James I, from whom Jamestown was named.

In 1617 they were in Gravesend preparing to sail back to Virginia, when Pocahontas died. She was buried in the town's

Church of St George, while Rolfe boarded ship with his son. He was to die in 1622 in the Massacre of Henrico.

The *Pocahontas Memorial* was put in the church at Heacham in 1933; Heacham Hall burned down in 1941; the last Rolfe died in 1990, and so ends the story.

But have another look at the church. Note that the tower is in the central crossing, and wonder how its weight is supported. Now see the enormous buttress that has done the job since 1802. The single bell, cast in the 12th century, is probably the oldest in East Anglia and the brass chandeliers, given by the Rolfes, are a copy of those in St Mark's, Venice.

HEACHAM MISCELLANY. On Guy Fawkes's Day 1795, 110 poor farmers and 106 day labourers met in Heacham church to organise their labour and so claim a reasonable wage, although one presumes the farmers were paid on the results of their labour. And this was 39 years before the Tolpuddle Martyrs met. The Heacham attempt failed because the Anti-sedition Law was introduced that same month. Is it coincidence that Moss Evans, the former leader of the TGWU, moved to Heacham in 1987 and was elected district councillor in 1991?

Norfolk Lavender

§NORFOLK LAVENDER.

Roughly opposite the church is Caley Mill, home of England's only commercial lavender farm, although there's another on Jersey. Founded in 1932 on the perfect soil – sandy, of low fertility, and in an area of low rainfall – the company has several isolated fields in the area on which it grows a variety of plants for distillation of the oil, producing half a ton in a good year. French lavender farms around Grasse squeeze 1,000 tons a year.

The oil is produced by steam-heating the flowers and distilling the resulting liquid, which is sold in the company shop and in other retailers across the country, and is also sold for commercial use although one customer, Yardleys, is no more.

The Romans perfumed their bath water with lavender, and the plant's name comes from the Latin *lavare*, 'to wash'. The Tudors used lavender-flavoured charcoal as toothpaste, and with beeswax as a polish. Later the oil perfumed tobacco and soap, and you can use the flowerheads in an infusion to make lavender tea – but a little goes a *very* long way.

The lavender grounds are open, year-round, free, with guided tours in the summer; the gift shop and tearoom are open daily except Christmas and New Year, and the conservatory shop on site sells plants from Easter to September. There are coach trips to more-distant fields in high summer. Phone 01485.570384.

Heacham has a vast **beach** to north and south, of sandcastle quality inshore, giving way to mud at low water level, which can be a mile away – so don't get caught by the incoming tide. Caravan sites dominate the coastline inland of the creek, which was once Heacham Harbour. Today there's no access by boat to the sea.

SNETTISHAM

Snettisham is the village that has the quarry that yields the carrstone that's used around the district, and which forms the red rocks of Hunstanton's distinct cliffs. But the village has three tourist attractions as well.

§SNETTISHAM PARK, formerly Park Farm, is a genuine working farm that has successfully diversified. Its 329 acres include 150 acres of parkland where you can see lambing in March, the deer calving in June and July, go horse-riding anytime, or lose your children in the adventure playground or playbarn. It's open from lambing to harvest, and then some. And if you enjoyed those dear little deer, take some home. Venison is on sale. 01485.542425.

The long road down to the shore passes the **watermill**, *erected in a time of scarcity by public subscription for the benefit of the neighbourhood, 1800,* according to a sign on the front. Now restored, the mill again grinds wheat at selected times, and sells the flour. Show the children the Lego exhibition.

At the end of that long road is **SNETTISHAM COASTAL PARK,** an important wildlife refuge 1.8 miles long and covering 143 acres and removing human pressure from a fragile environment. The warden is usually on duty daily Apr-Sep, but the park is always open, with lavatories near the entrance and a hide midway along the 'blue trail'. Among the many birds you can see here in season are curlew, brent goose, heron, merganser, short-eared owl, sanderling, snipe, turnstone and widgeon.

With habitat ranging from reed to open water, you may also see a range of Lepidoptera including burnet moth, large hawk, meadow brown, orange tip, and small copper. The flora is mainly salt-tolerant, including sea-holly, sea-lavender and glasswort – samphire.

The **beach** is ideal for development as an estate of sandcastles, but two miles out at low water you have ingredients for mud pies. There is no beach south of the village as the Great Ouse mudflats come this far. <u>Beware going out too far as the tide comes in faster than you can walk.</u>

The village's fourth attraction is in the British Museum: it's a gold bracelet of around 70BC which was found here. Man has probably lived on this spot since Neolithic times.

THE NORTH COAST
HOLME next the SEA

THE MOST FAMOUS LANDMARK at Holme isn't here at all – yet. It was discovered when an exceptionally low tide showed that the top layer of sand had been scoured from the beach, revealing a circle of 55 waterworn wooden stakes surrounding an upturned tree stump, its rudimentary roots paying obeisance to the heavens. Popularly known as **SEAHENGE**, the 4,000-year-old timber circle of unknown function was taken to Flag Fen, near Peterborough, for preservation.

Holme is otherwise known as the northern end of **Peddars' Way**, a Roman road coming in an almost straight line from **Castle Acre** deep in Norfolk, but it can be traced back to Knettishall near Thetford and we know it began at Camulodunum, today's Colchester. From Holme one presumes a ferry operated to near Gibraltar Point in Lincolnshire, for the track continues straight on to Lindum – Lincoln.

The village's Church of St Mary has a tower 76 feet tall and almost separated from the nave, which is austere inside. Built by Henry Notingham – one 't' – who was a judge to Henry IV, it was always too big for the village. In 1778 much of the nave was demolished, resulting in today's bizarre plan. Notingham's brass is the main feature of interest as it proclaims

Henry Notingham and his wife lyne here
Pat (that=who) maden this chirche stepull & quere (choir)
two vestments and belles they made also
christ hem save therefore ffro wo (woe = disaster)
and to bring her saules to blis of heaven
sayth pater & ave with mylde steven

There is no longer a stepull and the Notinghams' graves are outside as the church vanished from over them.

Ann Jane le Clerc of this parish had a daughter who married into the family of Lord Nelson. But Ann was a niece of General le Clerc, uncle by marriage to Napoleon Bonaparte, Nelson's enemy.

The village has an observatory run by the Norfolk Ornithologists' Association, with the Norfolk Wildlife Trust reserve nearby.

THORNHAM

Boadicea, or Boudicca, queen of the Iceni, destroyed Colchester in 62. The Roman governor Paullus retaliated, killing 80,000 Britons, after which Boadicea took her own life. The Romans colonised East Anglia, building forts – including one at Thornham. Its ruins were discovered in 1948 by a study of aerial photos, but a few artefacts have also been found. Excavations soon revealed a Saxon cemetery with 22 skeletons, all of which went to the Castle Museum, Norwich.

The Saxons began All Saints' Church – their porch and the priest room above it, remain – but most of the present work came after the Black Death of 1348-50. Thornham's mass grave for plague victims (1665) is by Staithe Lane, leading to the harbour. And a 'staithe' is a wharf or landing-stage especially for handling merchandise: it's a common word in the eastern counties.

Neglect hit the church. By 1845 the roof had collapsed and the bell was in the churchyard, but by 1900 the restoration was complete. A large colony of bats moved in after World War Two so the vicar and congregation ignored the Sixth Commandment, *thou shalt not kill*, and attacked them with tennis rackets. Thankfully, attitudes have changed.

A windmill and separate watermill were on Staithe Lane in the 13th century. Both have gone, but a model of the windmill was left in the church.

Henry VIII's dissolution of the monasteries in 1536 saw the seizure of Thornham Manor, which he gave to his physician, William Butts, co-founder of the Royal College of Surgeons.

The Hogge family who built Thornham Hall in 1788, ended with a daughter who married into the Ames Lyde family. She did the unthinkable for 1887 by starting **an iron foundry** in the village. Surprisingly, it survived, but never paid its way for several years. Then, in 1899 25 men were producing, among other things, small gates for Sandringham House and decorations for Balmoral Castle, and the next year they were making gates for the Royal Pavilion at the Paris Exhibition, and soon orders came from around the Empire. In 1914 Mrs Ames Lyde died and the Great War started, each a fatal blow to the business. The smithy closed in 1920 and was later the local service station.

The 16th century Lifeboat Inn, whose name marks the coming of the Hunstanton lifeboat, was a working farmhouse for generations and qualified to become an alehouse as it had a window opening onto the road, a strange ruling before Town and Country Planning was thought up. As smuggling was rife, the village had customs men in lodgings, some inevitably staying at the inn.

The **beach** is difficult to reach along a mile of the Norfolk Coastal Path and is therefore empty, but excellent.

TITCHWELL MARSH RSPB RESERVE

The RSPB bought marshland at Titchwell in 1973 to protect the rare Montague's Harrier, but the bird went away. In the next ten years sea walls were built, plus a car park, visitor centre with shop, toilets and hides, and now more than 100,000 visitors come each year to watch birds. The 940 acres include freshwater and tidal reedbeds and lagoons, saltmarsh and sand dunes, with more than 250 species recorded and 60 of them breeding.

With the decline of reedbeds in Britain, the associated birds have had a hard time. The very rare bittern bred here until the late 1980s, and returned in 2004, but the bearded tit has maintained its 20 pairs population; the other rarity is the migrant marsh harrier. Butterflies, moths, and the water vole – Ratty, of *The Wind in the Willows* – also thrive here.

The village has an excellent **beach** with parts of a so-called **petrified forest** (but it isn't *really* turned to stone) visible at very low tide. The church has a round tower, but there's stone from Normandy in the window surrounds. Is it a Norman tower in Saxon style or a Saxon tower with Norman additions? Nobody knows.

§BRANCASTER and SCOLT HEAD ISLAND

This beautiful village, whose name may mean 'burned castle', knows nothing of its Roman origins and lives by tourism and shell-fishing. The 14th century church of St Mary the Virgin is a copy of the one that Edgar the Peaceful (959-975) gave to Ramsey Abbey, and has a seven-foot telescopic font cover. Elsewhere a plaque recalls the village's lifeboats, *Joseph and Mary* (1874-93, saved three), *Alfred S Gerith* (1893-1914, saved six) and the final one, *Winalton*, which never saved anybody.

Little is visible now of the Roman fort at **Branodunum**, built to suppress the Iceni, and it was not until 1960 that the Romano-British cemetery was discovered nearby.

The hamlet **BRANCASTER STAITHE**, now bigger than Brancaster itself, developed as Scolt Head Island grew, and flourished in the 18th and 19th centuries. In 1797 it had a malt-house, claimed to be England's largest, but it was demolished in 1878. Sailing ships moved grain, coal and malt, but today the harbour is devoted to pleasure boats.

Continued on page 50

WELLS and WALSINGHAM LIGHT RAILWAY

The light railway is of 10¼ inch gauge and ran its first service in March 1982 along the route of the Wells & Fakenham Railway which suffered the Beeching axe in 1964. The new line is proud to claim the title of the world's longest railway of this gauge.

British Rail took up the track and sold the land, so the WWLR had to start almost at the beginning, even to moving 3,000 tons of rubbish from a cutting and spreading the remainder, leaving a 1:29 gradient, among the steepest for trains in Britain. The line started with one locomotive, *Pilgrim*, an 0-6-0 side-tank engine with two cylinders working to 125psi (8 bar), custom-built by David King of North Walsham. It had to haul four coaches with 42 passengers up that gradient.

The line succeeded and a fifth carriage was added in 1985, giving a payload of 52 passengers but taking *Pilgrim* to its limits. Soon *Weasel*, an 0-6-0 powered by a Ford diesel engine came, followed in 1986 by another steam loco, the *Norfolk Hero*, which is a 2-6-0 plus 0-2-6 with a Garrett loco and built specially for this line. Its four cylinders take 140psi and it's 20ft 4in long by 2ft 10in wide.

The service covers its four miles of track in 25 minutes on a season lasting Easter to September, with up to six return trips a day.

The WWLR runs a support group which organises activities on the line, arranges fund-raising, publicity and the purchase of new rolling stock; managing the shop at the Wells signal box, and organises volunteers to man the line. The season runs daily from Good Friday to the end of October; more facts on 01328.711630.

Wells & Walsingham Light Railway

Beans Seal trips

BEANS' BOAT TRIPS

These boat trips through Blakeney Harbour to the sandbank breeding grounds of Norfolk's seals, began in 1938 with Trip and Kitch Bean skippering the craft, and the business is now run by their sons John and Graham Bean and *their* three sons.

They run four motor-powered boats each carrying between 25 and 40 people and sailing every day from 1 April to 1 November, and at least twice a week in the remainder of the year, times always subject to tides and, occasionally, weather. Christmas and New Year sailings, subject to tides, last an hour, all others last two hours.

Sailings are ALWAYS from Morston Quay, accessible down a side road off the A149 near Morston Hall. Tickets must be collected from the house on the main road near the turning half an hour before sailing. There is a public toilet by the car park. And light snacks and drinks are available from the café on the quay.

At Blakeney Point we always see the seals hauled out on the sandbanks and we are able to sail very close to them and spend a half hour watching them watching us, and going to the old lifeboat house, depending on tides we are able to land passengers for up to an hour. Don't forget to bring your camera.

Common seal pups are seen in July and August, the greys from mid-November to mid-January and in summer we can see terns and many other species of birds nesting, but as their 'scrapes' are very vulnerable, visitors are not allowed to walk there, and dogs are allowed on a lead.

All boats – and Beans do not have the monopoly – are approved by the Marine Coastguard Agency, and all carry lifejackets. Tickets must be booked by telephone and paid for 30 minutes before sailing: contact John Bean at 12 The Street, Morston, on 01263.740038. Fax:01263.741306 or Graham Bean at 69 Morston Rd., Blakeney on 01263.740505

Mussels are still farmed in the harbour, brought here for three years from The Wash to mature, and whelks are dredged from the seabed 15 miles away. Samphire grows here in large quantity but, as some of the beds are protected, ask before you pick.

A good road leads to the beach, with a pay carpark, where the sand is perfect, and you could, if you're lucky, find remains of that same forest spilled over from Titchwell. The east coast of England is slowly sinking, regardless of what global warming may be up to, and this, plus Seahenge from Holme, can be considered the strongest evidence.

The **National Trust**, which owns almost everything between the coastal path and the low water mark, from Brancaster to Burnham Market, has an information centre at the staithe, open March to August, but times vary. Cycle hire is available at daily or weekly rates, and contact the call centre on 0870.458.4411 for renting self-catering accommodation anywhere in the country.

§ SCOLT HEAD ISLAND
and a geology lesson

This remarkable island is around 3.7 miles long and has been growing westward throughout recorded history. Its northern coast is a series of sand dunes protecting the salt marsh and running almost in a straight line from Overy Creek, which drains Burnham Overy Staithe. It is uninhabited and seldom visited, essential as its ecology is so fragile. A study of the map will show that it has been built up from sand and gravel eroded from the coast east to Weybourne and carried *westward* here by currents which stick close to the coast. Two children who drowned recently at Holme were carried to near Weybourne, showing that there is a counter-current running *eastward* but a bit further out. This counter-current merges with the main flood coming down the east coast of Britain and is responsible for the Holderness Peninsula in Yorkshire, and Orford Ness. At Weybourne, the westward current is no more and the main current scours the coast on its way east: this is why, from this village on, the cliffs are being eroded and the beach is narrow.

But back to Scolt Head Island. The National Trust bought it from Lord Leicester of Holkham Hall in 1923, with the Norfolk Naturalist Trust buying the eastern tip in 1945; the Nature Conservancy Council leased the entire island for 99 years in 1953.

Here is England's largest breeding colony of sandwich terns; there are other tern species, gulls, plovers, oystercatchers, *et cetera*. A marked trail assures minimum disturbance by the likes of us, with dogs banned from April to August. The ternery is closed in May and June because, if you were to walk there then, you would never see a tern's nest. It doesn't make one; it lays its eggs in a scrape in the sand and it takes a clever gull to separate egg from shingle.

When there is access, it's from Brancaster Staithe, depending on tides and weather.

INLAND FROM HUNSTANTON

The largest inland village for miles was once called **'Dry' DOCKING** as it is on a hilltop almost 300 feet above sea level, with no permanent stream nearer than Fring. The villagers dug a well in 1760 and at 237 feet they struck water, which was then sold at a farthing a bucket. Hauling up the water must have been a thirst-making task, but it was not until 1928 that a pump was installed. It proved so erratic that in 1934 people bought water from Bircham Newton airfield at a ha'penny a bucket.

The oldest part of St Mary the Virgin's church is the chancel, built before the Black Death, but an earlier church may have had links with Aelfric, Bishop of Elmham, in 1038. As a Norman order of monks owned Docking rectory in 1415, Henry, fresh from the Battle of Agincourt and distrusting the French, seized it for the Crown, where it stayed until Henry VI gave it to Eton College.

STANHOE is a tiny village, but its 14th century church of All Saints has a wall tablet remembering Sir William Hoste of Burnham Market who fought in the Battle of Lissa (Croatia, 1866). It doesn't explain why he was there, or why the main hostelry in **Burnham Market** is called the Hoste Arms. I can tell you. Sir William was born in the Burnhams in 1780 and served under Nelson in several campaigns. The 17th century hotel in Burnham Market was built to serve people coming to the local assizes and was a staging post on the roundabout coaching run from Lynn to Norwich.

OTHER VILLAGES. Poor Fring's only claim to fame is that it was mentioned in Domesday – but so was **Sedgeford**, where the Saxon church's round tower has survived, entombed in the later square tower. **Ringstead** has one of those rare Norman round towers on St Peter's Church; it's now the only part that survives, in the grounds of the former rectory. That was Ringstead Magna; Ringstead Parva and its church of St Andrew have completely disappeared and the dedication to St Andrew has been transferred to Ringstead Magna.

Or maybe landscape is more to your interest? The road from Ringstead to Holme offers some splendid views across The Wash, and on a clear day you can see the Lincolnshire Wolds.

The Poppy Line, the North Norfolk Railway

WELLS – NEXT – THE – SEA
NELSON'S NORFOLK

WELLS MADE MUCH of its living in medieval times by plundering shipwrecks. As the definition of a wreck was a vessel on which nobody had survived, those men first at the scene often had some unpleasant business to do, and Wells men acquired the nickname of *bite-fingers* for their time-saving method of removing rings from corpses.

Although it is only '*next*-the-sea' *with* the hyphens, Wells has lived on maritime trade until recent times, with the earliest mention in the 13th century. The north Norfolk ports, including Blakeney and Cley, could manage vessels up to 160 tons – and, for scale, that was larger than any of Columbus's three ships as the *Santa María* displaced only 90 tons.

An Act of Parliament in 1675 created the Wells **Harbour Commissioners** who could then charge 6d (2½p) for every tun or last loaded. A tun was 252 gallons if wine, less if beer, and a last was 640 gallons of grain. If you've forgotten, a gallon is what petrol used to be sold in. An Act of 1835 changed the duty to a shilling (5p) a *ton*, not 'tun', of the ship's registered tonnage.

An Act of 1844 allowed the commissioners to buy property and thus build the present quay, which meant the demolition of 28 cottages and sheds. The same Act decreed that a lifeboat be provided, with a £2 a day fine if it were not seaworthy: this rule continued until the RNLI brought its own boat in 1869.

Back in 1758 one Sir John Turner began draining the marshes by Warham, but in 1858-59 the Admiralty gave Lord Leicester of Holkham Hall permission to build a **sea wall** north from town – it's where the harbour railway runs – cutting off 588 acres of marsh, as well as tidal access to Holkham village. As a result, Holkham harbour died and Wells showed signs of terminal illness when the silt began piling up: as the sea wall was dead straight it cut off the flow of water westwards, and nature does not like straight lines.

But silting never conquered Wells and the port continued trading despite the prognosis. Indeed, it prospered from 1850 to 1914, although the railway took some business from 1857. Cargoes were mainly coal, malt, and barley, with Guinness long a buyer of the malt. Trade stalled during the Kaiser's war, and after 1918 changed to potash in and sugar beet out.

Hitler's war stopped almost all activity as Wells became an Air-Sea Rescue base. Whelk fishing recovered quickly after the war, with Wells supplying sixty percent of the nation's needs, but general trade was in the doldrums with around 14 ships a year using the place. Favor Parker bought the quayside in the 1970s and increased the import of animal fodder, but exports were still slack.

Examples? In 1965 there were 248 shiploads in, totalling nearly 100,000 tons – but nine shiploads out, at 4,150 tons. In 1968, 218 shiploads in and the final one out. Hereafter, with imports only, the balance of trade was one-sided, but in 1989 there were 121 in, in 1990 51 in, in 1993 and '94 18 in each year.

The problems are twofold. There is a draft limit of ten feet, attainable only on spring tides – and dredging is uneconomic. It's the chicken-and-egg business again but, as Scolt Head Island shows, silting is inevitable. In a thousand years Wells could be two miles inland.

But **private boating** is on the increase, with many permanent moorings in the outflow creek. Boats capable of more than 15 knots are allowed in harbour only for shore access and all craft must obey the 5mph speed limit. Jet skiing is banned in the harbour, and windsurfers must have a licence. At the outflow's end, skiers and windsurfers are allowed, but only in designated areas. **The channel current is fast**, so weak swimmers must be careful.

As Wells has the only *commercial* harbour between Lynn and Yarmouth, it is popular with private yachtsmen on passage. But naval vessels have cause to remember Wells: *Tuesday, 27 February 1898. The naval gunboat* Alarm *heaves to and launches its shoreboat. Shoreboat overturns in rough seas. Six men drown. Coastguard boat goes to rescue, capsizes. Five more drowned. Eleven men therefore die in an exercise to deliver a copper lamp to the harbourmaster.*

Further disasters are recorded on Favor Parker's silo on the quay, which carries flood markers for 11 January 1978 (16ft 1in above high tide) and 31 January 1953 (16ft 10in, the notorious east coast floods, when a ship was lifted onto the quay.) These same dates are also recorded at King's Lynn's Church of St Margaret.

Wells Museum, which opened in 1991 behind the Harbourmaster's office, has photos of the stranded ship among many

54

maritime exhibits, but it's moving to a newly-built Heritage Centre, so it will be leaving its neighbour, a box on a pillar, which is almost a museum exhibit in itself. The box is the National Rivers Authority's **tide measure**, which relays information by phone.

There was another disaster in January 2005 when the harbour-front amusement arcade was destroyed by fire.

§ RAILWAYS

Beside the tide measure along Lord Leicester's sea wall is one of Wells's two 10¼inch gauge railways, owned by the same man. The **Harbour Railway** runs from near the museum to the coastguard lookout and lifeboat station by the beach – there's also a good pay car park here. Trains operate Apr-Sep with up to 18 return trips a day, serving Pinewood Caravan Park or anybody who wants a ride. The **beach**, by the way, is one of the best in England, and is an official Area of Outstanding Natural Beauty consisting of beautiful pinewoods and sand dunes pegged by marram grass, planted by the Coke family of Holkham Hall. There are no services at all, but that's as it should be.

Crabbing in Wells-next-the-Sea

For the second track, the Wells & Walsing-ham Light Railway, see page 48.

A "PINK FOOT"NOTE

Wells was probably the best place for wildfowling a century ago, and it was popular with the aristocracy who took up to 15,000 pink-footed geese in a season off the marshes. Wildlife should be thankful for these, more enlightened times.

SANTA CLAUS

Wells's patron saint is **Nicholas**, who cares for children, fishermen, pawnbrokers, merchants, travellers, and a few other categories. He was the original Santa Claus, a name which is corrupted from the Dutch *Sint Niklaas*. Old Nick gave three bags of gold to pay for the marriage of the daughter of a Turkish merchant who had fallen on hard times – hence today's pawnbroking sign. He's supposed to have tossed the money down the chimney – hence the legend of Santa Claus. And it happened in Myra, near Antalya in Turkey, because Nicholas was its Christian bishop and died there around 324.

So what's the connection with Wells? The church is dedicated to Santa Claus – Saint Nicholas.

The first known church on this site was built around 1229, the first known vicar came in 1302, and the place was rebuilt around 1460. Then in 1879 lightning struck the tower, and the church was burned out. St Nicholas's was rebuilt by 1883 to the same design, at a phenomenal cost of £7,000.

Two objects that escaped the fire are a brass eagle-style lectern and the church chest. The lectern had vanished years before – hiding from Cromwell's men, perhaps – and was found buried in a field: a pickaxe made a hole in it. The chest still has scorch marks on it.

The parish register records the baptism of John Fryer, sailing master of HMS *Bounty*, made notorious by **Captain Bligh**. Fryer's headstone was removed and his grave is now lost.

§ HOLKHAM HALL

Let's begin with **Robert Coke**. Born in Mileham, near Fakenham, he was a lawyer at Lincoln's Inn. His son Edward, born in 1552, studied at Norwich and Cambridge. Called to the Bar, he later married Bridget Paston whose ancestors had written the **Paston letters**, England's earliest recorded diaries. He went on to buy **Godwick** Manor for £3,500 and built the elegant Godwick Hall. Bridget soon died in childbirth so Edward, now knighted, married the wealthy widow of Sir William Hatton who created **Hatton Garden** in London. As if that didn't keep Sir Edward sufficiently busy, he also led the trials of **Sir Walter Raleigh** and Guido Fawkes – **Guy Fawkes**.

Eventually the family produced **Thomas Coke** who did the Grand Tour then in 1718 decided to build the ultimate mansion on the family estates at Holkham. He didn't start straight away and he didn't choose to build at Godwick, as the village had died around 1600 from poor harvests on poor land, and Sir Edward's hall was then in ruins: it was demolished in 1962. (In fact nowadays the only building standing in the **ghost village** of Godwick is a bit of the church.)

Now let's move to the **Earldom of Leicester**, a title held by Simon de Montfort among others. Several families qualified for the earldom and it eventually passed to Thomas Coke who, by now, had started work by planting the avenue of beeches at Holkham. Soon the hall was to be built and, in time, the estate would grow to 3,200 acres (exactly five square miles) and be part-surrounded by a brick wall nine miles long.

Thomas died in 1759 and the now-completed *hall* passed in 1766 to **THOMAS WILLIAM COKE,** born 1754 – but the *earldom* passed to the **Townshend** family. Thomas William C. became Member of Parliament the year he inherited Holkham, and he stayed there with few breaks until 1833. Let us digress again, for in his years at the hall he established his reputation as **Coke of Norfolk,** the man who devised the four-year cycle of crop rotation: wheat, turnips, barley-with-clover, clover on its own. Modern gardeners have a different system, but this rotation introduced a forage crop and a root crop, so livestock could be kept overwinter instead of being slaughtered in the autumn and salted. The extra dung increased fertility and turnips soon appeared on cottage tables.

Yet he couldn't have done it alone. **Charles Townshend** of Raynham Hall (in Norfolk, but a bit outside our coverage area), whose family had picked up the Earldom of Leicester, and was soon to lose it, had studied turnip and clover cultivation in the Netherlands and so given Coke his raw materials. Charles T. was brother-in-law of **Robert Walpole** (oh, how intertwined this story gets!) but he – Charles – is better known as **TURNIP TOWNSHEND.** His grandson, also Charles, when he became Chancellor of the Exchequer was famous for imposing taxes on the New England colonists and so prompting the **Boston Tea Party**, but that's another story, thank goodness!

Both Robert Walpole and Charles Townshend owed part of their success to **JETHRO TULL**, who invented the horse-drawn seed drill. And all three relied on the final collapse of the feudal **strip system**, in favour of a man owning a set piece of land outright and not holding it by grace and favour from the lord of the manor. Parliament had already passed the Enclosures Act which brought major changes to the countryside: hedges now separated the smaller fields, and cottages went up on the new holdings. Half the farmland had been enclosed by 1750 and statistics show the results. In 1700 England produced 13,000,000 quarters of wheat, but in 1820 the yield was 25,000,000. A quarter? That was 64 gallons. There were many factors leading to this increase, but pride in ownership of the land was certainly one of them.

Let's just go back to Thomas William Coke to tidy up some loose ends. In 1837 he got hold of the Leicester earldom and in June 1842 he died. He's buried in **Tittleshall** Church which still survives though it's very close to Godwick. You can read about Tittleshall later; it's a bit too much to put in here.

§ HOLKHAM HALL TODAY

And now let's go back to the hall itself. It is among England's most majestic of stately homes. Indeed, it's difficult to decide which is more impressive, the lavish building or its contents, which include many works by Gainsborough, Rubens, Van Dyck, and others. The **alabaster entrance hall** is a masterpiece which sets the tone of what is to follow as you walk through room after room, seeing exquisite furniture and enormous tapestries. There are thousands of adjectives in the dictionary, and you are at liberty to select from them at your leisure, but they may not be strong enough. At one time the library here at Holkham grew so big that many books had to be moved, and the Bodleian at Oxford took them, yet despite this the collection here is still one of Britain's biggest.

When Thomas Coke died, his widow, the Countess of Leicester commissioned 'Capability' Brown to design the **ornamental gardens.** Brown was so much in demand that he made a vast fortune, but the grounds at Holkham show he had great skill as well. Today the six-acre walled kitchen garden, still holding the orangery and vinery, grows roses, alpines, bedding plants and pot plants for sale, and is open year-round, Mon-Sat, afternoons. 01328.710424.

The vast collection of old household items that featured on Anglia Television's **_Bygones_** programmes is permanently housed in Holkham's converted stables. You can find steam engines and fire engines, motor bikes and milk churns, a smithy and a laundry, and much else besides. Other attractions include a **gift shop**, Easter-Oct, a display of the **History of Farming**, and a **cruise** on the park's lake in an electrically-powered launch. For information, call 01328.710424, for voice mail information.

The village of Holkham clusters around the entrance to the long drive, but **St Withburga's Church** is inside the encircling wall. It stands on a mound built by the Saxons, hinting that a Saxon chapel was here. The plaques inside indicate the church is very much a memorial to the Coke family.

The BURNHAMS and LORD NELSON

There are at least six villages called Burnham Something. There's §**Burnham Market**, the main village above the tiny River Burn; **Burnham Overy Staithe**, where yachts can moor, *staithe* meaning a mooring-place; **Burnham Overy Town**, which is no larger than a hamlet; **Burnham Deepdale**, no bigger; **Burnham Norton**, the 'north town' of the group; and **Burnham Thorpe**, birthplace of Admiral Horatio Nelson. Old Ordnance Survey maps mark Burnham Westgate, Burnham Sutton and Burnham Ulph. The last two are in the parish of Burnham Sutton-cum-Ulph.

Let's look at **BURNHAM THORPE,** to the south-west of the collection. There's not a lot to see, but All Saints' Church has a checkerboard finish on the east wall. So what, you may ask. A similar design is on the heraldic shield of Sir William Calthorpe in the chancel floor, inferring that Sir William financed the east wall. The Calthorpes also left their mark on the churches at Anmer, East Barsham, and Cockthorpe.

The crest of H.M.S. *Nelson* of WW2 is on an interior wall, and her flag is in the north aisle with that of H.M.S. *Indomitable* of WW1. An ensign of the Nelson era flies from the tower on suitable days; the rood was a gift from Canada in Nelson's honour, while the cross and lectern were made from wood from H.M.S. *Victory*. The great chest was made from the Rev Edmund Nelson's pulpit, and the hassocks show *Victory* under full sail. Finally, a bust of Nelson is on the chancel wall.

LORD NELSON

Edmund Nelson was curate at Beccles in 1744 when he met Catherine Suckling, great-niece of Sir Robert Walpole. After their marriage they moved to Downham Market and from there to **Burnham Thorpe** in 1755. The sixth of their eleven children was **Horatio**, born 29 September 1758 in a house called the Shooting

The Hoste Arms, Burnham Market

Box. He was seven weeks premature and baptised within hours as nobody thought he would live.

The young Horatio studied in Norwich then moved to the Paston Grammar School in North Walsham as its owner was a friend of Mrs Catherine Nelson, who had recently died; no great surprise after eleven children. A year into Paston School he heard that his uncle had been appointed captain of H.M.S. *Raisonnable*, so Nelson begged his father to let him join the Navy as 'captain's servant.'

Nelson's early career took him to the West Indies and the East Indies, the Arctic and the Mediterranean, seldom coming back to Norfolk. He was commander of the *Boreas* when he met Fanny Nisbet on Nevis in the West Indies, and they married in 1787.

Horatio and his wife came home soon after; he opted for half pay and spent five years at Burnham Thorpe, sometimes visiting Houghton and Holkham halls. At last he was listed as captain of the *Agamemnon* in 1793, bound for the Med, where he met Lady Hamilton at the Court of Naples. It was the beginning of one of the best-known love affairs in history.

He lost his right eye in 1794 off Corsica and his right arm in 1797 off Tenerife, but in the process he became a national hero, a Knight of the Order of the Bath, and Rear Admiral of the Blue – at the age of 38. He came home to Burnham where Fanny nursed him for seven months, then he went off to the Battle of the Nile and earned the title of Baron Nelson of the Nile and Burnham Thorpe. His final battle was off Cape Trafalgar, a headland in south-west Spain, on 21st October 1805 where he was killed, aged 48 years and 22 days. His body was shipped to Gibraltar where it was put in a barrel of brandy for preservation, then home to England.

But not for interment at Burnham: he was destined for the crypt at St Pauls.

The Government gave Nelson's two surviving sisters £1,000 each; his elder brother received an earldom, £6,000 a year, and £100,000 to buy an estate, an over-generous award and an indication that sexism ran rife. Lady Nelson received a pension of £2,000 a year – and Lady Hamilton got nothing; she died destitute in 1815. The nation got Nelson's Column in Trafalgar Square and another in Great Yarmouth.

THE *OTHER* LORD NELSON

The only pub in Burnham Thorpe is the §*Lord Nelson*, which was built in 1637 as *The Plough*. It was in advanced decay but still trading when Les Winter took it over in 1966. He restored it to 1793 standards and made it into a Nelson museum, retaining the old settles (high-backed bench seating) among other items. Winter's conclusion was that Nelson's private life was in such a mess – Lady Hamilton had borne him an illegitimate son – that he dressed in his finery to advertise himself, and begged to be killed at Trafalgar. It is possible, as his final words to one of his captains *before* the battle, had been: "God bless you, Blackwood. I shall never see you again." Or was he psychic?

The pub that bears his name was honoured as Pub-Restaurant of the Year (for Norfolk) in 1994; it has an AA rosette for food, and the landlords, David and Penny Thorley, sell their own labelled brandies, *Nelson's Blood* and *Lady Hamilton.*

THE OTHER BURNHAMS

St Mary's Church in §**Burnham Deepdale** has a Saxon round tower of around 1040; the single bell was cast in Lynn in the 14th century. The Norman font was damaged during restoration in 1791 and spent forty years in the garden of Fincham Rectory. Now restored, its 12 panels show the farming year from the labourer's point of view.

Now, isn't that strange in these days? A village, about which I can find nothing to say except its church, almost a thousand years old? That sums up many parts of rural Norfolk, especially along this coast. I *don't* mean it's backward – I mean it's unspoiled, a relic of bygone ages.

St Margaret's Church in **Burnham Norton** also has a round tower – so is it Saxon? There are deep architectural debates, but the concensus is that the tower dates from around 1090. The nave and chancel are Early English and Perpendicular, taking them into the 15th century, and the impression is that the interior would make a wonderful setting for a medieval film, except for the modern pews.

This church has other marvels: a bread oven in the north porch; the Jacobean pulpit has been claimed to be the best in England; and for most of its life the church had two rectors jointly appointed, making it a 'mediety'; and it's a mile from the village because the people abandoned the old community during the Black Death.

Sir William Calthorpe, of whom we've heard, helped found the Carmelite Friary in Burnham Norton in 1241; its name comes from Mount Carmel, near Haifa. The white-robed friars thrived, extended their home in 1249 and 1353, and at the dissolution in 1538 it owned 68 acres – but the four remaining friars were broke. Lady Anne Calthorpe wanted to buy the place but Thomas Cromwell, Earl of Essex, first stripped out the lead, silverware, and the bells. The ruins passed to the Pepys family, relatives of Samuel, then to the Walpoles, and finally the Cokes. Today it is an insignificant ruin by the school.

Two rectors for one church? At **Burnham Sutton-cum-Ulph** we have two churches for one rector and one parish, in an age when that was unusual. The name is easy. Ulf was a Dane who owned the manor, and Sutton is opposite to Norton.

The Church of St Mary the Virgin at **Burnham Westgate** has a tower built around 1310, and there's a window in memory of Sir William Boulton, a frequent benefactor to Nelson.

Burnham Overy provides another example of a mobile village. The community began around St Clement's Church in **Burnham Overy Town**, but as the Burn silted, seagoing vessels had to moor progressively further downstream and eventually most people were living at **Burnham Overy Staithe**. St Clement's was an oddity: its tower was at the crossing but as it was too heavy for the walls the arches were bricked in, giving the feeling of two naves sharing a tower.

There are three **mills** in Burnham Overy; a private watermill on the B1155, and the beautiful §National Trust mill on the A149 where the 18th century buildings include a malting floor. The last is a windmill built in 1816 and restored in 1980. None is open to the public.

Sir William Hoste, born in the Burnhams in 1780, served under Nelson in several campaigns and, as we have seen, is remembered in a plaque in Stanhoe church. The §**Hoste Arms** is the smartest hotel in the conglomeration of villages and predates Nelson. It was built to serve people coming to the local assizes, and was also a staging post on the coaching run circuitously connecting Lynn and Norwich.

The CREAKES

Strange that two groups of nearby villages should be named from alternative names for 'river', particularly when they cluster around the same stream. But, then, running water is at a premium in Norfolk. The B1355 passes close to the ruins of *Creake Abbey,* an Augustinian community founded by Sir Robert de Narford and his wife in 1206. In 1504 all the priests died of the plague in one week, and the abbey ceased to function. It's now owned by English Heritage and is permanently open, free.

The Church of St Mary the Virgin in *NORTH CREAKE* is probably 12th century, and the dedication is to the *birth* of Mary, while St Mary's in South Creake concentrates on her *assumption.* The nave is large and high, with an impressive hammer-beam roof, and traces of the rood stair remaining. Several surviving wills mention bequests for work on the tower – for instance, Nicholas Aleyn (Allen?) left £20 in 1435, Margaret Jaye left 26/8d (£1.33) in 1450, and Margaret Forster added 10/- (50p) for the bells in 1470 – yet none of those bells predates 1744 by when inflation had done its work on the cash.

Yet another Sir William Calthorpe is shown in a large brass of around 1505, holding a model of the church which he rebuilt.

The Rev Thomas Keppell, rector from 1844 to '63, served under **Captain Frederick Marryatt** who wrote novels, notably the classic *Masterman Ready* (1841) in which Keppell was the model for Mr Midshipman Easy.

63

The old village forge in Church Street has survived as a living **museum** of the blacksmith's art. In this rambling flint smithy the old-style coke forge is still heated by bellows, and old-time tools still hang on the walls. The tea rooms offer blacksmiths' lunches, and the River Burn runs through the tea gardens. Open weekdays in summer.

At the south end of **SOUTH CREAKE** County Crafts mounts a permanent exhibition of paintings by local artists, and sells local craftware.

EAST FROM WELLS

The Burnhams have prepared us for that Norfolk phenomenon of having more churches than there are villages, but the village of **WARHAM** went to the extreme and had *three* churches, all at the same time. **St Mary Magdalene** is the main one, amid the lime trees – you can easily miss the gateway. **All Saints** is a towerless church to the east, and **St Mary the Virgin** was to the west, but only the foundations remain. In addition, records mention a chapel. The answer to all this is easy: there were once three villages.

All over Norfolk, and into Suffolk, we can see evidence of a declining population. The reason is obvious: in the days when wool was king and the Industrial Revolution was years into the future, the eastern counties were the most densely peopled part of the country, excluding the immediate conurbation of London – but that wasn't enormous. When wool went it killed not only the sheep-rearing jobs but the spinning and weaving as well, both of them cottage industries until Manchester and the mill towns took over. That's why there's only one city of any size in Norfolk, and why there's a liberal scattering of tiny villages. As farm work became mechanised in the 1950s, there was yet another drift from the land, until light industry moved in to stem the flood. Between the wars a farm might employ fifty men, and many of their wives on a part-time basis, but in the mechanical age two men, or even the farmer and his family, can do the same jobs. Godwick certainly isn't the only ghost village, but it shows why all of Norfolk is relatively unspoiled.

St Mary Magdalene has traces of Norman work in an arch, but building continued until the 15th century. If you appreciate medieval architecture, look at the priest's door to the chancel, set in

64

an inverted Y buttress. The interior is strikingly simple, with the box pews still in place.

The list of incumbent priests is almost complete from 1278. Every one until 1377 has a name with the French *de*, 'of', in front of it. This shows the Norman domination from 1066, fading gradually as the English language emerged from the mix of Norman and Saxon. By the way, the list includes Thomas Robert Keppel with one 'l'; here he was in charge of the combined parish of St Mary Magdalene and St Mary the Virgin from 1837. All Saints was a separate village until long after WW2.

Do you realise that the English language was created on the landed estates? The Saxon labourers, speaking Low German (I shall use modern German), would know their livestock as *living* stock: *Kuh* for cow, *Schaf* for sheep, *Huhn* for hen, *Schwein* for pig. Norman owners, speaking French, knew their animals only as *dead* stock served at meals: *bœuf* for cow, *mouton* for sheep, *poulaille* for poultry and *porc* for pig. It shows who was who!

But back to Warham. The chapel is a testimony to the **Turner** family whom we met in King's Lynn. Charles Turner became brother-in-law to Prime Minister Walpole, and his brother John was one of Lynn's two MPs 'keeping the seat warm' for Walpole while he was in the Tower of London. If you don't believe this, read the inscription on John's tomb.

There were times when both Lynn seats were held by Turners. The family bought the Warham estate in 1709 but in 1604 it was owned by Thomas Howard, the Earl of Surrey who was beheaded that year. Howard's tomb in Framlingham Church is claimed to be the most heavily-gilded *in Europe*. The last of the Turners died in 1780 and five years later the celebrated Coke of Norfolk bought the estate and demolished the hall. His last words are claimed to be about his two regrets in life: the demolition, and allowing hay-making on a Sunday.

Go south from All Saints' and look for a footpath sign at the crest of a hill. A cart track leads to the vast double-ring earthwork of §**Warham Camp**, covering several acres and with mounds thirty feet high. Iron Age relics were found here in 1959, plus a Saxon midden. It's on private land but you can visit it at any time. And south of Warham lies **Wigton** with its School House Art Gallery.

Everybody knows that §**STIFFKEY** is pronounced *stewkey*. Well, it isn't. The locals call it how it's spelled, and that's good enough for me. *STEWKEY* was the 16th-century spelling and pronunciation but, stiff or stew, it's a charming little village once dominated by Stiffkey Hall, which the Bacon family began in 1578. At its prime, around 1650, the hall had 80 rooms but most of it was destroyed by fire in the 18th century: remains include the west wing and a gatehouse dated 1604.

The village had a church in 1066 – but which one? St Mary's, as now is, was built around 1310 and a second church, that of St John the Baptist, was added in the 15th century – each with its own rector. It's an ecclesiastical version of the parliamentary rotten borough. St Mary's was demolished in 1558 – you can see a trace of it in the churchyard – and St John's was extended. But which church stood on the original site?

South of Stiffkey is the tiny village of **COCKTHORPE**, whose church of St Andrew and All Saints is redundant, but a sign says where you can borrow the key. The church was built of rubble, and plastered, showing a lack of funds. The inside is equally plain and simple, and there's another tomb to another of the prestigious Calthorpe family – Sir James, who died in 1615. His wife, born Barbara Bacon, is remembered in a wall plaque which explains that *by her he had 8 sons and 6 daughters, in whose several marriages and issues the ancient glory of the name and family…did reflourish and is dilated into many of the best houses in the county.*

When Barbara died at the incredible age of 96 she had 193 descendants. Also verging on the incredible.

Two English admirals were baptised in this poor church: **Sir John Narborough** who served under Blakeney man Sir Christopher Myngs in the Battle of North Foreland in July 1666. The other was **Sir Cloudisley Shovell**, who sailed under both Myngs and Narborough. He helped in the capture of Gibraltar in 1704 but his ship, the *Association*, was wrecked in the Scillies in 1707. In 1737 a dying woman confessed that Shovell was washed ashore alive, but she killed him for the emerald ring on his finger.

Cloudisley Shovell was reputedly born at Cockthorpe Hall, a 16th-century house in brick and flint that held a toy museum, but it's now closed.

LANGHAM

On the further side of the wartime Cockthorpe airfield, now used in livestock rearing, is Langham, a small village that was known as **Langham Episcopi** after Pope Alexander III gave it to the Bishop of Elmham in 1176. Most of the present church is 15th century on 14th century foundations. It was originally dedicated to St Mary in 1603 but after a bishop of Norwich wrote that it was *whollie ruynatd and p'faned long since*, restoration began and St Andrew was added to the patronage. Two of the three bells were cast in Blakeney in 1699 and 1702 – a strange place to find a bell-foundry.

Do you wonder why this book talks so much about churches? Just look at the skyline and you'll see the most dominant things are – churches.

So here's a change from that subject. The novelist **Captain Marryatt** lived in the village from 1843 to '48, and was lost at sea on 20 December of that year.

Here's something else. Go a little way north from the central crossroads and you'll find §**LANGHAM GLASS** in the flint Long Barn, built in 1722 for Langham Hall Farm. In 1981 it was converted for Langham Glass, a workshop where one can see quality crystal glassware blown and moulded. The owners claim this is probably the only house in the country making glass in commercial quantities by hand. A ton of molten material is used each week, the special sand and other chemicals being heated for 7^1/$_2$ hours overnight in excess of 1,300°C, and the products are sold world-wide. Open year-round with demonstrations at limited times in summer. 01328.830511.

MORSTON

The people of the coastal village of Morston believed in the Second Coming of Christ. Proof? When the tower of the 13th-century Church of All Saints was shattered by lightning in 1743, the villagers saw no need to repair it, for wasn't Christ due back quite soon? Only when they realised that Christ was not on the next bus did they do the work.

Or was there some other reason? Were they too poor? Or were they too stingy? Were they prepared to let the newly-arrived Saviour see his house in a mess?

Inside, look for the carving on the first corbel on the left, which shows the village gossip with his – or her – tongue out. The church is noticeably poorer than the Cley, Blakeney, and Wiveton trio, where there was much better access to the sea and its riches in the Middle Ages. So *did* they believe in the Second Coming?

A lane leads to Morston Quay where you can join a boat to see the §**seals** on the sandbanks: there's also the chance to visit Blakeney Point depending on season, tide and weather.

For information on Beans' Boat trips to the seal colonies, see page 49

BLAKENEY and BLAKENEY POINT

Where is Snitterlea? The Domesday records of 1086 refer to a settlement called **Esnuterle** or **Snuterlea,** meaning 'on a bleak location'. From this came the Middle English verb *sniteren*, 'to snow', and *Snitterlea*, presumably the 'village in the snow'. (Let's forget that *-lea* means 'meadow' as it only complicates the issue.) But where is - or was - Snitterlea? There has been no coastal erosion here since the retreat of the glaciers, yet there's no trace of a settlement on a bleak location.

The name *Blakeneye*, probably meaning 'black island', appeared in 1230, and in the 14th and 15th centuries the village was known as *Blakeney* and *Snitterlea*. (Now let's remember that every placename in East Anglia which ends in *-ey* or *-ea* [but not

The Blakeney Hotel

-lea] shows its Norse origins, as this suffix means 'island.') Finally, the names divided and Snitterlea became the manor, church, or friary, and Blakeney became the harbour. My theory was that the village was built on high land to the south, bleak in the winter winds, and the 'black island' could have been the growing Blakeney Point.

But some people think the name came from Blekinge in south Sweden! I pass.

The fact remains that Snitterlea–Blakeney was a busy medieval port, sending grain, and salt from the pans at **Salthouse**, in return for fish. Henry III granted Snitterlea a market in 1223, and in 1326 Blakeney was one of the country's 59 ports permitted to trade in horses, money, and precious metals, which was an honour.

Edward III controlled the sale of fish at Snitterlea in 1358 as there was a big market at Blakeney; after this, the Blakeney name took precedence.

The size of the village's **Church of St Nicholas** infers that the community prospered. The nave was rebuilt around 1435, making it distinctive from the earlier chancel. At the same time the great west tower was added, 104ft tall – but some sources claim 120 ft. One bell survives, cast in 1699 – the same year as one of the Langham bells. But the strange thing about St Nicholas's is its *eastern* tower, probably built along with the friary. Was it a lighthouse, as it's visible 20 miles out? But the other tower is taller. Was it a belltower? But the other tower is stronger.

Parish records were in fair detail from 1538, but interesting marginal notes come from 1727 to 1781, when Henry Calthorpe (*with* an –e) was rector. He noted the 'Great Snow' of five hours on 3 May 1698, the storm of 28 October 1772 when hailstones in Blakeney were '4 inches in girth' and the 7ft sturgeon caught in Blakeney Pit, the channel north of Morston.

Blakeney's nave probably served the village while the chancel served a **Carmelite Friary**, established in 1296 and completed in 1321. The friary was north of the windmill – which is not a tourist attraction – on the site now occupied by Friary Farm.

Little is known of this friary, but St Nicholas's chancel has a brass plaque bearing a Latin inscription, which reads in English: 𝔥𝔢𝔯𝔢 𝔩𝔦𝔢 𝔱𝔥𝔢 𝔟𝔬𝔡𝔦𝔢𝔰 𝔬𝔣 𝔍𝔬𝔥𝔫 𝔠𝔞𝔩𝔱𝔥𝔬𝔯𝔭, 𝔨𝔫𝔦𝔤𝔥𝔱, 𝔬𝔫𝔢 𝔬𝔣 𝔱𝔥𝔢 𝔣𝔬𝔲𝔫𝔡𝔢𝔯𝔰 (a mistake; it should read 'benefactors') 𝔬𝔣 𝔱𝔥𝔢 𝔠𝔬𝔫𝔳𝔢𝔫𝔱 𝔬𝔣 𝔣𝔯𝔦𝔞𝔯𝔰, 𝔞𝔫𝔡 𝔬𝔣 𝔄𝔩𝔦𝔠𝔢 𝔥𝔦𝔰 𝔴𝔦𝔣𝔢, 𝔴𝔥𝔬 𝔡𝔦𝔢𝔡 𝔱𝔥𝔢 16𝔱𝔥 𝔡𝔞𝔶 𝔬𝔣 𝔄𝔲𝔤𝔲𝔰𝔱 𝔄𝔇1508. It's the Calthorps again! Sir John's will of 1503 states that **his Synnfull body was to be beryed in the White ffryes of Sniterlie, that is to say in the myddys of the chancel.** (I daren't give you too much old English script) And that's where he is.

The best-known associate of the friary was Sir John de Baconsthorpe, born 1290, educated at the friary and later found practising medicine in Paris. But, of course, you've never heard of him.

The Census of 1580 gave Blakeney's population at 360, with the village owning 12 ships of tonnage ranging from 16 to 100; Wiveton had 13 ships, the smallest of 40 tons; and Cley, with 450 people, had nine ships for fishing off Iceland.

THE SPANISH ARMADA. The Privy Council, through the Mayor of Lynn, requested the three villages to provide a vessel or supplies to be sent against the approaching Spanish Armada in 1588. One story claims the trio refused the request, not so much from defiance of a royal demand but suspecting extortion from Lynn. Another version claims all the men were away fishing off Iceland, while a third story grants that Blakeney and Cley agreed to contribute, but Wiveton didn't.

We can be sure that the seamen of the three villages enjoyed a reputation in high places: the fishermen were exempt from the Press Gangs which snatched men off the streets for indefinite military service without the option

By the early 16th century the Dutchman van Hasedunck had been commissioned to *reclaim the marshes* at **Salthouse**, prompting Sir Henry Calthorpe to build a causeway from Blakeney to Cley, thus cutting Wiveton from access to the sea. After local protest the Privy Council ordered the bank to be destroyed – but it was too late to save Wiveton. Then in the 17th century the bank was rebuilt, from Salthouse to Blakeney Point, so enclosing the harbour for evermore. The resulting silting of the Glaven gradually killed the commercial traffic, although Blakeney managed to ship coal and grain until 1914.

Near the village centre and near the seafront is Blakeney's so-called §GUILDHALL, a 14th-century building that's now owned by English Heritage and is open during the day, free. The main feature is the undercroft – cellar – where you have an early example of a brick-built vaulted ceiling. This is all that remains, but it's highly unlikely to have been part of a guildhall. Nearby is the Guild of Many Crafts, which exhibits and sells samples of embroidery, paintings, needlework, woodcarving, and other handicrafts.

The quayside **Blakeney Hotel**, the undisputed centrepiece of the village and opened in 1923, replaced the Crown & Anchor pub, which the locals called the Barking Dickey. The Manor Hotel began life simply as the Manor House.

The Norfolk Association For Saving The Lives Of Shipwrecked Mariners introduced an oar-driven lifeboat around 1820, based on Blakeney Point for a speedy response, though there could be delays in getting to the point; in 1860 eight men drowned in the harbour when answering a call. The RNLI took over the station in 1861 but closed it.

§ BLAKENEY POINT

The founders of the **Norfolk Wildlife Trust** bought 407 acres of Cley marshes in 1926. This, with the National Trust sector, puts the entire coastline and point under protection. Access to the point is by boat from Morston or on foot along the bank from Cley. The peninsula is forever changing its shape and is slowly expanding westward. At least 256 species of bird have been seen on the point, including terns, plovers, avocets, bittern, and Lapland bunting. The point is also a vital feeding-ground for spring and autumn migrants. The colony of seals was reduced from around 700 to 200 by the epidemic of 1988, but it has completely recovered.

Blakeney Point claims an impressive list of flora as well, with more than 190 flowering species recorded.

WIVETON

The stone §**bridge** near Wiveton's **Church of St Mary the Virgin**, has long marked the head of navigation of the Glaven River, for it was <u>built in 1292 and is still in use</u>. Its builder, William Storm, put a wooden bridge in Cley in the same year, but that, of course, hasn't survived.

The church has several recently-discovered masons' marks showing sailing ships, and parish records name some of the actual vessels: the *Gyles*, the *Gift of God*, the *Trinity*, the *Confidence*, and the *Mary James*. They ranged from fishing boats and merchant ships to men-of-war.

The church, built at the head of the harbour late in the 13th century, now overlooks the village green. A John Hakon wrote in his will of 1437 that he left 200 marks (£132 at the time) for 'þe makyng of a newe chyrche in Wyveton.' The letter þ (lower case) is the old way of writing soft *th* as in 'the', and we'll meet it again.

But back to Hakon's extremely generous bequest: in 1482 a shipowner left 8d (3.5p) as a contribution 'for the bells' and his widow left 6d for their repair. A Robert Paston (remember that name) left money to repair the chapel on the stone bridge, and traces of the little building survive to this day, on the bridge's south-west corner, despite the heavy lorries which trundle over.

Legend tells of a baby boy found on the green in the 16th century. Orphaned, he was brought up by the entire village to share the cost. He was given the name **Raul Greneway** and, says the legend, he became a rich merchant and founder of the Greneway Charity which left money for the local poor. The charity survives, but the legend was wrong. Greneway was the son of a local farmer and merchant, and his brass in the church has the Greneway arms, the Grocers' Company arms, and his merchant's mark. His treasure chest and the Greneway charity date from 1558, the year of his death and the start of parish records.

Wiveton is overshadowed by its neighbours and no visitor would suspect its past glories, but listen to the story of **Susan**, *a good shippe of burthen...pressed into Queen Elizabeth's service in 1588 for service into Portugal, of which Thomas Coe of Claye went as Quartermaster.* Coe claimed the village had 19 other good shippes, six having been built in the village.

An old document states that the Lord of Wiveton Dulcis *hath a bushel of coals, salt, or any measurable thing, of every ship that doth unload within the precincts of that manor.* In addition, English ships paid 4d to anchor, and foreigners 8d (19p). You could say that the aristocracy would go to any length to extract a tax.

CLEY NEXT THE SEA

The Church of §**St Margaret of Antioch** is at the southern tip of Cley, surprisingly close to Wiveton church, with Blakeney church nearby; you can also see Glandford church to the south. What was I saying about churches? St Margaret's is impressively large for a tiny village, the nave and side chapels being 65ft by 115ft, plus 28ft to the altar rail. The tower is short because it belonged to the earlier church on this site.

Sir John de Vaux had been granted 'Cly' Manor in 1265 as he already held Boston in Lincolnshire, then England's second-largest port – he presumably travelled between the ports by boat for the road journey would take him way south of Cambridge. Maritime trade was growing steadily, and after his death in 1288 his daughters rebuilt the church. John Ramsey, a master mason of Norwich, was in charge of the work and in 18 years of intermittent labour he produced the masterpiece still evident: the five-leaf-clover windows are based on those in

Cley-next-the-Sea's narrow street

the Palace of Westminster – or so it is claimed.

When Lady Petronella de Nerford (Narford?), de Vaux's elder daughter, died in 1326, Ramsey retired and the proposed new tower was abandoned, although his nephew continued with lesser work until the **Black Death** killed him in 1348.

The §South Porch, added after the Black Death, is a masterpiece of masonry. Look for the 16 armorial crests and, in the roof, an old woman throwing her distaff at a fox that has stolen a chicken. There's no link, but it leads me on to **Old Woman's Lane**, a road that runs north-and-south just to the east of Cley. It takes its name from the story, which may be true, of the elderly female who hanged herself from one of the ash trees beside the lane.

Cley is another village that moved. A major fire in September 1612 destroyed 117 houses around the church but, as the Glaven was already silting, the new houses were built a little to the north, with further growth taking the village ever northward.

Local seamen captured a Scottish ship in March 1406, taking Prince James of Scotland to France. As England and Scotland were temporarily at peace, the 11-year-old prince was sent on to London where Henry IV held him hostage until war should break out again: kidnapping and piracy have never been far removed from the affairs of Norfolk seamen. The *Norfolk Chronicle* reported in December 1824:

> *Thursday and Friday last, were seized on the beach and afloat, by the officers of His Majesty's Customs at this port (Cley) 120 half-ankers of Geneva, 19 bags of tobacco, 10 bags of snuff, 10 boxes of segars, and two Chinese ornaments.*

73

The same paper recorded in 1883 a gunfight at Weybourne between smugglers and customs officers, who seized 127 half-ankers of brandy and 3,500 pounds of tobacco. An anker? Call it a gallon.

MODERN CLEY

Cley today is a beautiful village troubled only by a narrow street and a tight corner – and the threat of flooding, but this has largely been relieved by an unobtrusive sea wall. Along the main street is *Made in Cley*, a group of potters who make their wares on the premises, and their puns as well. And have a look at the Post Office whose front wall appears to be built of animal bones. The nearby Smoke House is a handy stop-off for smoked fish and other foods. The **beach** is mainly shingle, but there's a handy pay car-park.

§ CLEY MILL, the artists' delight and a some-time continuity shot on BBC TV with a passing hot-air balloon (why ever did they stop screening it?), was begun in 1713 and the best-known miller was the last, Steven Barnabus Burroughs, who worked it from 1840 to 1919 – 79 years. In 1921 it became a holiday home, renovated in 1983, and it was caught in the 1953 floods, losing much furniture in the ebb tide. It is now open to visitors daily Easter to Sep, and the original stables are now self-catering apartments. A mile east is a Norfolk Naturalists' Trust observatory for watching migratory birds; it's also the visitor centre for Cley Marshes, open most days in summer, and with a convenient car park.

GLANDFORD

Don't miss Glandford. It has one of the most picturesque §**fords** in Norfolk. At the end of WW2 the county had hundreds of fords, most of which have succumbed to bridges. Glandford survived. The ford over the Glaven is around 100 feet wide and normally too deep for cars, although four-wheel-drives can cross. There is a bridge for pedestrians.... and photographers.

All but one farmhouse and a few cottages was rebuilt early in the 20th century by *Sir Alfred Joddrell* of Bayfield Hall to the south. He even rebuilt §**St Martin's Church**, which was in ruins in 1730. Then along came Sir Alfred who demolished all but the chancel and rebuilt it to his own design, between 1899 and 1906.

This is no ordinary church. It's a miniature. From inside it looks like an oversized doll's house, yet it has everything a parish church should have: hammerbeam roof, rood screen, carved pulpit – all carved from local oak and cedar. The carvers even put each other at opposite ends of the frieze above the pew behind the door.

Nearby is the §**Shell Museum**, which Sir Alfred built in 1915, and now holds exhibits from around the world. Open on irregular hours, the museum is well worth a visit. Have you met a nautilus elsewhere in Norfolk?

South of Glandford on the banks of the Glaven lies **Natural Surroundings**, the Wildflower and Countryside Centre with 8 acres of open woodland devoted to the countryside as it used to be. You can see red squirrels (the young are released in Anglesey), harvest mice, nightingales on Kelling Heath, Highland cattle, 100 species of wildflowers and almost every specie of native British tree.

There's a full calendar of activities for all ages, craft courses, and everything designed to let modern man – and school parties – know what's missing. With testimonials such as *"you inspire us with wonderful ideas"* it's a breath of rural nostalgia. www.naturalsurroundings.org. uk or 01263.711091.

Little Walsingham Art & Crafts Centre

WALSINGHAM TO CROMER
HOLY NORFOLK

WALSINGHAM IS ENGLAND'S NATIONAL SHRINE. In medieval times it was the most important pilgrimage site in northern Europe, and a rival to Santiago de Compostela in Spain, and even to Rome. It died completely with the Reformation but its revival began in 1829, and Walsingham is now back on the pilgrimage and tourist trail. Tens of thousands come each year, notably at Easter, but it cannot rival Knock in Ireland, Lourdes, Fâtima in Portugal, or Santiago. If you're looking for it on the map, try LITTLE Walsingham. Great Walsingham is a mile away and somewhat smaller.

Now it so happens that *Lady Richeldis de Faverches,* pious owner of the manor of Walsingham, had a vision of the Virgin Mary. In a dream she was taken to Nazareth of a thousand years earlier and shown the House of the Annunciation, where Mary had heard of the baby she was to bear. Don't snigger: it could have been a genuine out-of-the-body experience, especially when you learn that Lady Richeldis had the vision twice more, convincing her she was to build a replica of Christ's home here in Walsingham.

She ordered a small timber chapel to be built between two wells, but unseen forces prevented the work. Lady Richeldis spent the night in prayer and in the morning the chapel was built – on another site.

Much later, the Fransiscans built their priory at the south end of the village, and Elizabeth, Countess of Clare, founded the Augustinian Priory of St Mary in 1347 on the site of Lady Richeldis's original chapel. Both orders served the pilgrims who came to Walsingham, as it was much safer and cheaper than going to the real Nazareth. Soon, indeed, Walsingham became known as ENGLAND'S NAZARETH, drawing pilgrims from hundreds of miles away.

Look at the Ordnance Survey map and you can see the tracks those pilgrims made from King's Lynn and Heacham, from Burnham Thorpe, Wells, and Blakeney. Many miles of these paths survive today, and many other miles are the modern tarred roads.

Henry III made a pilgrimage to the **Priory of Bromholm** at Bacton in 1233 as, ten years earlier, the priory, an extension of §**Castle Acre,** had claimed to have a fragment of the True Cross. The publicity was good, as the Miller's Wife in the *Canterbury Tales* calls: *"Helpe, Holy Cross of Bromholme!"* Other abbeys made the same claim (there being enough fragments around the world to make *ten* crosses), so Walsingham counter-claimed to have a sample of mother's milk from the Virgin Mary! So great was this absurd claim that for ages the Milky Way, in the night sky, was known as the Walsingham Way! Oh, yes – in 1241 Henry II came to Walsingham, the first of ten visits.

Walsingham even influenced politics when Edward I and the Count of Flanders signed a treaty of alliance here in 1296. Much later, as Catherine of Aragon's sons had not survived infancy, Henry VIII made a barefoot pilgrimage to the holy shrine to pray for his ailing son. The baby died. Henry decided it was Catherine's fault and so began his campaign for divorce, which led to the break with Rome and the *dissolution of the monasteries*, initially affecting all orders with an income greater than £200 a year. Walsingham was valued at £391.

The priory was wrecked. Sub-prior Nicholas Mileham and layman George Guisborough were executed. The Walsingham Madonna was taken to Chelsea and burned. By 1538 it was all over. Walsingham, and almost all other monasteries, nunneries and abbeys were ruined. Only the §**great arch** of the priory's east window remained – as it still does, behind locked doors (if you can't get in, peer through the gap in the door, and if you get in in February you'll see the country's greatest display of **snowdrops**). Walsingham languished for almost three centuries until in 1829 came the Catholic emancipation, and in 1833 a group of Oxford intellectuals planned the Second Reformation: it became known as the *Oxford Movement.*

Soon, a few pilgrims were returning to Walsingham, even though almost everything was in ruins. But Charlotte Pearson Boyd bought the derelict 14th-century **Slipper Chapel** in Houghton St Giles (1½ miles south), and restoration was complete by 1934. Originally the final stopping-place for pilgrims from the south, it is now the **Catholic National Shrine** holding the **Holy Ghost** chapel.

Pilgrims were coming in numbers by 1897, slowly building up to 10,000 in one procession in 1934. (On these narrow roads!) In 1938 the Holy House and well were incorporated in the **Pilgrimage Church** which has fifteen side chapels. The pilgrimages ceased during WW2 but on 17 May 1945, six days after the German surrender, the U S Army Air Force in Norfolk organised the first Mass at Walsingham since the Second Reformation.

The rate of rebuilding accelerated. Meanwhile, a duplicate of Lady Richeldis's shrine had been built in Buxted, Sussex, in 1887, inspiring the local lad Alfred Hope Patten to devote his life to re-creating Walsingham. He became a priest, was offered the Norfolk parish in 1921, and stayed until his death in 1958. He had achieved his ambition by rebuilding Lady Richeldis's shrine here in 1931, discovering one of the wells in the process. The chapel, now the §**Holy House**, holds the

Grand Annunciation Altar, based on the original priory seal held in the British Museum. This is the focal point

Shrine of Our Lady of Walsingham

of religious life in modern Walsingham and the start and finish point of all pilgrimages.

Steps beside the Holy House lead down to the §**Holy Well** where pilgrims are once again baptised, and many claim to have spiritual healing – see the plaques of appreciation.

Mass is held daily at 7.30 a.m. in the shrine, 11.30 in the chapel, and Shrine Prayers are offered at 6 p.m. There are many other prayers, plus services at the Slipper Chapel, the Methodist and Catholic churches, the parish church of St Mary and All Saints, and the Russian Orthodox Church in the former railway station. There are summertime candlelit processions at 8.15 p.m., but the most spectacular are at the **National Pilgrimage** each Spring Bank Holiday when thousands of people attend.

SECULAR WALSINGHAM

Little Walsingham was a small farming village until the revival of England's Nazareth, and it has adapted to its new role while retaining all its charm and character; the only modern housing is tucked out of sight. A tour of the village on foot could start at the §**Shrine Church**, from where we go north along Knight Street, passing the §**Refectory of the College of Clergy,** a half-timbered 16th century house. Left into Guild St for **Guild House** at the next junction. A right fork leads to Egmere Road and the terminus of the

W&WLR; there's no station.

Left takes you south into Bridewell St and the open area of §**Common Place**. On your right is an alley leading to the former §**prison**, built in 1787 on the site of a former leper hospital. A 'bridewell' is a prison, taking its name from the jail which stood near St Bride's Well in London. Come to think of it, there was a prison in Clink Street as well. The Walsingham bridewell had four treadmills, and it's open at irregular dates.

Opposite the alley is a 15th century building, now a shop, beside which is the **Shrine Office** which arranges pilgrimages and accommodation: the 16th century §**pump house** is closed but can still draw water. At the bottom of Common Place is the 15th century Bull Inn while on the south side, behind the limited parking space, is the §**Shirehall Museum** and **Tourist Office**. The museum holds a courthouse of the time of George III. The property is under the same administration as Cromer Museum and the tourist office is the agency for guided tours of the village.

A walk down High Street is a visit to a living tableau of architecture from the 15th to the 18th centuries, plus the Georgian front of number 33 and the 13th century gateway leading to the few remains of the priory, open April to September, limited days. There's also the country's only Grade I listed public lavatory.

An alley, right, leads to the **Market Place** and the 15th century **Black Lion** hotel. The south end of Market Place rejoins High Street by the Methodist Chapel, built in 1794, then you are faced with a Y-fork. Left, Church Street leads, of course, to the parish church, damaged by fire in July 1961 but restored. Right, the main road leads to the §**Slipper Chapel**, with a side road to the ruins of the **Fransiscan Friary**, another of the buildings that Henry knocked about a bit.

GREAT WALSINGHAM

Overshadowed by its neighbour, Great Walsingham's §**Church of St Peter** is worth a visit, but the village's tourist interest is the **Textile Centre,** the old name under which an Arts and Crafts business now trades. One part holds a tea room selling drinks and cakes, as well as pottery and gifts. The other side of the business has regular exhibitions of sculpture, pottery, jewellery and oriental carpets and is open 363 days a year.

Continued on page 82

SHERINGHAM MAZE & GARDENS

The Maze and Gardens at Beeston Regis, Sheringham, offer an enjoyable day out for all the family. An oasis of peace and tranquillity between the sea and the coast road, it provides inspiration for the garden, plant and beauty lover.

Priory M&G is very much an atmospheric garden, with an increasing range of unusual plants which are more or less hardy to the locality. With natural running water, wild flower meadows, woodlands, and the newly-built romantic garden and grass & bamboo garden, a wonderful ambience of unspoiled countryside is experienced, which provides that priceless feeling of relaxation and escape.

The countless butterflies and moths, insects, birds and other small creatures also provide an excellent learning place for children from 3 to 103, and which leave them with a lasting souvenir of an enjoyable day.

We also have the only traditional hedge maze in Norfolk, formed by 10ft clipped copper beech and hornbeam. Nearby is a Christmas tree block maze, which features our Christmas maze and quiz trail to find Santa's Grotto.

The gardens were begun in 1985; the mazes were planted in 1990, and all opened to the public in 1998, and the incredibly mild microclimate has helped everything to mature quickly.

Foxgloves Tea Room and restaurant caters for garden visitors and passing public with a full range of morning coffee, lunches, cream teas, or a full meal. We serve weekend breakfasts from 9 to 11.

Our plant centre has a range of unusual items from around the world, many of them 'grown on' here. We also have urns and planters. We hold events in the grounds, from gardeners' evenings to jazz, mostly with a meal. Phone 01263.822986 or visit our website **at www.priorymazegardens.com**

Sheringham Maze & Gardens

Sheringham Park

SHERINGHAM PARK: National Trust

Designed in 1812 by Humphry Repton, Sheringham Park, which holds Sheringham Hall, was created by the Upcher family between 1813 and 1839. The park is one of the renowned landscape gardener's most outstanding achievements; the large woodland garden, introduced later, is famous for its spectacular show of azaleas and rhododendrons in the peak flowering time of May and June.

There are stunning views over the park and along the north Norfolk coast from the viewing towers, particularly from the pagoda, where visitors look out from a platform level with the tops of the surrounding oak trees. There are many way-marked paths and boardwalks through the woods and park and along the cliffs close to Sheringham town, making the grounds the ideal place to enjoy a gentle stroll or a brisk walk at any time of year.

Many visitors enjoy a trip on the North Norfolk Railway, and Weybourne station is just a short walk from the park.

National Trust Sign

The Hall is leased to a tenant but is open to visitors between April and September following written agreement with the leaseholder. There is a car-park charge, but entry is free for National Trust members.New visitor facilities were opened for the 2005 season, with a shop, café-style catering, and an exhibition about the creation of the park, and the Upcher family who planted the woodland, and their links with Sheringham and its lifeboat.

BINHAM

Binham had a **§priory** that outshone the Augustinian one in Little Walsingham, and even in decay its ruins are impressive, the nave still serving as the parish **§Church of St Mary.**

And how about a potted history lesson? Pierre de Valoines, nephew of William the Conqueror, founded the priory in 1091 as a dependency of the Benedictine Abbey of St Albans; Henry I endowed it around 1104 and the first prior, Osgod, came in 1106 although the nave was not begun until 1130 and work was to last 150 years.

The Abbot of St Albans sacked Binham's prior, Thomas, but his friend Robert Fitzwalter declared himself patron and refused to accept the dismissal. The abbot laid siege to the priory in 1212, forcing the monks to starvation level and, when King John heard of the trouble and sent troops, Fitzwalter fled.

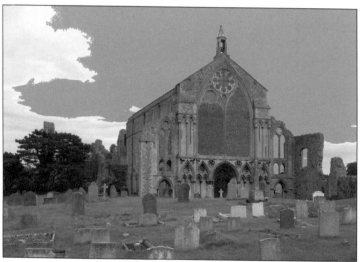

Priory church of St Mary and Holy Cross, Binham

A generation later the monk Alexander de Langley drove himself mad through too much study. The prior flogged him, and ultimately buried his body in chains.

Richard de Parco, 1227-'44, was the only honourable prior. True, he raised a charge on Wells windmill to buy hassocks and asked another village to feed his monks when the larder was empty, but he did much restoration, and still had £20 when he left office.

But most others were downright crooks with William de Somerton (1317-'35) the worst. He sold the silver and spent the money on trying to turn base metal into gold, stupid man. He was imprisoned, escaped, rearrested, then fled, leaving a debt of £600. At the dissolution in 1540 the annual income was down to £140.

Henry VIII gave the ruined priory to Thomas Paston in 1542, and the **Paston Letters** record the receipt in 1553 of 13 shillings 7½ pence for rubble to build a house in Wells. Paston wanted to build himself a house here, but when falling masonry killed a labourer, his workmates saw it as an evil omen.

Restoration was in progress in 1715, and in 1809 the enormous west window opening was bricked up for safety; it had the earliest example of bar tracery in England.

Today, most outbuildings are down to ground level, leaving only the nave – but what a nave! It's an enormous parish church, and also holds a bat colony. English Heritage owns it but there's no entry fee.

English Heritage also owns the damaged *Market Cross* on the green, site of an annual four-day fair from Henry I's time to the 1950s.

NORTH ELMHAM

St Augustine brought Christianity to England in 597 (don't confuse him with a namesake of 354-430) and became first Archbishop of Canterbury. St Felix – remember Babingley? – was first Bishop of East Anglia from 631, his bishop's see based at the great port of **Dunwich**. About 680 the area was split, roughly on the lines of the *North Folk* and the *South Folk*, with the northern diocese centred on **Elmham**. This endured until the Viking attacks and the slaughter of St Edmund in 870. Then Alfred defeated the Viking King Guthrum (Goturm) who converted to Christ and made Dunwich his capital city and bishopric.

Elmham was demoted. When the See of Norfolk was reinstated, the bishop moved to **Thetford** in 1071 – and Dunwich gave way to **Bury St Edmunds**. But in 1085 the honour passed to Norwich, where it has stayed.

For ages the Elmham ruins were forgotten, called locally the '*Castle Hills*.' An amateur digger in 1870 assumed they were 14th century; in 1903 they were thought to be Saxon, and in 1962 this was proved. Finally, the **§ruins of Elmham** came to light in 1967, with still later work dating the masonry to between 1090 and 1120. But this date was *after* the bishopric moved to Thetford! In fact, the demoted cathedral was built of wood: this stone structure was North Elmham's Bishop's Chapel – with 14th century additions as at first supposed.

Henry le Despenser, Bishop of Norwich in 1370, helped put down the **Peasants' Revolt** in 1381 and in return was given the chapel at Elmham, which he converted into a moated and fortified house. He scattered many human skeletons in the process, but his work preserved Norman masonry that would otherwise have been lost. The place was abandoned when he died in 1404, and lay forgotten until 1948. It is now under English Heritage control, open any time, free.

Beside the chapel ruins is the elegant parish church, its oldest part being stones in the chancel from the time of Bishop de Losinga. The chancel was in ruins by 1277 but was restored in the 15th century. The tall tower is in three stages, and for a small fee you may climb it, for some good views. Now here's an oddity: the church (that is, the font) is dedicated to St Mary, but the south chapel is for St James and the north for St John. Such multiple dedications infer the church was important.

BILLINGFORD lies two miles east, site of a Roman settlement on the ancient road from Caister to Castle Acre, and a major crossing point of the Wensum in Saxon times. The Billinga family founded the Royal House of Saxony and was prominent in the 11th century.

§PENSTHORPE WATERFOWL PARK

A mile or so east of Thetford on the flood plain of the River Wensum, stands a 200-acre park for wildlife, offering woodland, wetland, meadow, and flooded diggings from which a million tons of gravel have been raised. Now more than a hundred bird species can be seen here, including king eiders from the Arctic and pygmy geese from the tropics, as well as scarlet ibis, avocets and ruffs. In the woods, long-tailed tits and nuthatches live while marsh marigold and marsh orchid are among the plants that find refuge. You may also be lucky enough to see a shrew or a stoat.

School parties are welcome at the World Education Centre, and there are art and craft exhibits in the courtyard gallery. Opening is restricted to weekends in winter, but the park is open daily in summer. 01328.851465.

§THURSFORD COLLECTION

Go several miles further east for the collection of steam engines and fairground attractions, and several Wurlitzer and other makes of organ, including an enormous §Mortier. This is the life's work of George Cushing who went to King's Lynn fair in 1920 and was fascinated by the lights and music. A few years later he bought his first steam engine and hired it out. He bought many more when petrol was replacing steam and these giant machines were selling at scrap value. George started steam rallies and the crowds came pouring in, and eventually his bizarre fleet became the *Thursford Collection,* based in the farm where he stored his first steam engine.

. When the Wurlitzer came from the Paramount Cinema in Leeds in 1976, it needed a special building, and in due course a special organist: Reginald Dixon, who had another such instrument at the Tower Ballroom, Blackpool. A resident organist now gives daily concerts each afternoon in season (April to October) and at the special Christmas carol concerts which have been featured on television. 01328.878477.

LITTLE SNORING

Apart from jokes about the village name (which comes from a Saxon invader or settler named *Snear*, meaning 'swift, alert' – anything but sleepy), Little Snoring is worth a visit for the sake of its church. §**St Andrew's** is unique. Its round tower is Saxon, probably from around 1010, and it stands separate from the nave – there are freestanding *square* towers at West Walton, Beccles and Dereham – and it still has its ancient dovecotes, from which birds would be taken for the table during lean winters.

The nave, too, predates the Norman Conquest, but all other masonry is no older than 1240. The bell was cast in 1770 and the organ was built around 1880 by an amateur in Fakenham. Restored in 1987 it is now of national significance.

The nave has another surprise: four notice boards from **R.A.F. Little Snoring**, a WW2 airfield nearby. Records of decorations begin with Sgt Rosenbloom's DFM in 1943 and end with W.O. Smith's DFC in 1945. Another board lists the enemy planes damaged or destroyed. A museum, an organ, an ancient nave, a freestanding tower: I said the place is unique.

BALE

You're too late to see the celebrated §**Bale Oak** in Bale or Bathley. It had a girth of 36 feet at human waist level and its longest branch stretched 75 feet when the tree was felled in 1860. It was condemned to death because the parish councillors refused to accept responsibility if the branches fell on anybody – and you thought the litigation society was modern! The lord of the manor, Sir Willoughby-Jones, had the timber hauled to Cramer Hall in Fakenham, in a great procession. And somebody, somewhere, counted a thousand rings.

Stories claim that twenty people could stand inside the hollow trunk, that a cobbler made it his home and that at another time people kept pigs there. The Bale Oak is believed to be the last relic of a Saxon or Celtic sacred grove, with All Saints' Church nearby for the holy link – the only stained glass there shows oak leaves and acorns. But the nicest touch is the notice on the site:

> Here I stand all in disgrace, once the wonder of this place.
> My head knocked off, my body dead,
> and all the virtue of my limbs is fled.

There's another notice in the church. It has no connection with the oak, but it's interesting for its possible once-libellous content:

Be it Remember'd That Thos Gay, bought of Lucy Clarke, with Bale Town Money which Sum was Sixteen Pounds Ten Shillings, A piece of Land laying in Wells… This Money was given by James Ringall to Buy Blankett to Clad the Poor of Bale, many Years Since. Anno 1774.

You can't libel the dead, but you can certainly carry a grudge.

GODWICK, the ghost village.

It's gone, except for a Tudor barn now part of a modern building, and the corner of the church. Look for the ruins at OS 955222.

The village sign at Bale shows two of the occupants of the hollow oak in days gone by: the cobbler at his last and the pig-keeper with some of his herd.

TITTLESHALL

We're getting far enough from *north* Norfolk now, but the **§Church of St Mary the Virgin** at Tittleshall is certainly something to see for its collection of tombs. Here lies *Sir Edward Coke* (see Holkham) whose memorial cost £400, and the tomb of his wife

Bridget, with eight of her ten children. A long plaque lists Coke's achievements, including Speaker of the House of Commons, Lord Chief Justice to James I – and prisoner in the Tower of London.

There's a memorial to great-grandson Robert Coke, grandfather to Coke of Norfolk, KB, Baron of Minster Lovell, Viscount of Holkham, Earl of Leicester, and builder of Holkham Hall. He was the last of the Cokes to be buried here, his funeral procession stretching 2½ miles, and the nave is overwhelmed by his magnificent memorial. His first wife Janet is remembered here, with a carving that cost 3,000 guineas (£3,150) in 1805. Sir Edward Coke was born in 1552 in the nearby village of Mileham. Stigand was lord

The Holkham Centre

of the manor here in 1043, when he became Bishop of Elmham. By early 1066 he was Archbishop of Canterbury and, as such, crowned King Harold who died at the Battle of Hastings. It was the Stigand link which prompted the Normans to build a castle here, but only the earthwork remains – on private land behind the village sign.

CROMER TO HAPPISBURGH
DISAPPEARING NORFOLK

THE SEA HAD CLAIMED the church of *Shipden-juxta-Mare* by 1390, so they built another at *Shipden-juxta-Felbrigg* on land given by Edward III. As the area was known as **Crowmere**, the new community took that name.

The **Church of Sts Peter and Paul** in CROMER was completed in Henry IV's reign, its tower, at 160 feet, being the tallest in Norfolk and an ideal landmark for seafarers. The church prospered for a mere century until Henry VIII's actions over the monasteries cut off further investment: an inventory of 1552 said that the five bells, weighing 62 cwt (3 tons, 16 stone), were valued at £46. 10s. (If you want it in today's speech, 3,149kg and £46.50p). The decay continued: in 1681 the chancel was so dilapidated that it was demolished by gunpowder; by 1757 the nave roof had collapsed, restricting services to the base of the tower. Ten years later the Bishop of Norwich sold the brasses and the roof lead, as well as four of the five bells. Legend claims the bells were sent by sea to their new home in St Mary le Bow Church, which could mean they became the famous **Bow Bells** – but the Whitechapel Foundry can prove that *it* cast the bells for St Mary le Bow and St Mary atte Bow.

Today the restored Cromer church has six bells weighing 2 tons 9 cwt 9lb, and a sign in the belfry states they are 77% copper and 23% tin.

At the 90th of the 171 steps in the tower (§ for view) is an opening called *Harry Yaxley's Hole*. A friend held Harry's legs as he dangled outside the hole, collecting birds' eggs. The friend demanded a greater share of the yield, but Harry called back: "You shan't hev 'em."

"Then I'll drop you."

"Drop away, then," said Harry – and reached the ground quicker than he expected. He survived.

Cromer grew slowly and was purely a fishing village until the unwanted railway began bringing tourists. As it had no harbour, all the boats were launched from the beach and hauled into town when storms threatened. The locals changed their ideas about the railway when it started carrying their crabs to a much wider market, including London. We have already seen that the special sea bed off the town is conducive to crabs; this geology is explained at the

§**Cromer Museum** on Tucker St near the church. The museum occupies a row of fishermen's cottages from Victorian times, and keeps the original fittings, as well as exhibiting a fishing boat in the yard. It's received a £500,000 improvement grant and is open daily. Come and see Britain's oldest elephant fossil found at West Runton.

The §**Lifeboat Museum** by the disused No 2 Lifeboat Station is open May to September and, not surprisingly, it tells the story of the Cromer lifeboats, from No1's first call-out in December 1867 to the brig *Wild Rose*, and it's still in service, launched from the end of the pier. No 2 was on station for a century, closing in 1967.

Talking of the pier brings to mind that it was cut in two in 1993 by a drilling rig which was drifting in a storm, but it was back in service by 1994. Lesser damage had been inflicted in 1953 and 1989. A talk of the lifeboat must bring **Henry Blogg** to mind. He joined the RNLI in 1894, aged 18, and retired 53 years and 9 months later, in September 1947, having been the coxswain for 37 years. He won the George Cross, the BEM, the RNLI gold medal three times, the silver medal four times, the Canine Defence League silver medal – and the Queen of the Netherlands presented him with a gold watch. He died in 1954.

From 1935 to 1945 he coxed the *H. F. Bailey* which answered 128 calls and saved 518 lives. Peter Cadbury of the chocolate company bought the boat in 1991 and presented it to the museum as its main exhibit.

RESORT RÉSUMÉ. Cromer is a picturesque town with its own distinct character. The town centre is on a moderately-high cliff looking down onto the **beach**, with a good sandcastle area at the top, and that chalk layer beneath. Entertainment is aimed at adults, and the town doesn't cater for the Benidorm or Blackpool set. It has a lively carnival in late May; for details ask the tourist office on Prince of Wales Road, 01263.512497.

OVERSTRAND – 'above the beach' – is a satellite village to the east. It has no promenade, no entertainment, and beach access is down steep paths cut by erosion in the cliff. The 14th century church vanished into the sea, so St Martin's is an 18th century replacement. The village is popular with retired people.

WEST RUNTON holds several camping and caravan sites on the clifftop to the west, with others hidden among the pleasant hills formed by glacial terminal moraines. The **beach** ranges from sand to shingle, with a large car park. Holy Trinity Church serves both East and West Runton, its 13th century tower being the oldest part, as the nave collapsed in the 14th century. It's been rebuilt. The main attraction is the –

§NORFOLK SHIRE HORSE CENTRE

which opened in 1982 as a working museum, not as a commercial farm – the only crops grown are for the animals. Twice daily (not Sat) in summer, David and Jonquil Bakewell have one or more of the centre's shire horses give cart rides for the children and – subject to the season – demonstrations of ploughing, drilling, harrowing, tedding (hay turning) and wheat harvesting, all done by horse-power, as it was before tractors took over in the '50s.

The shire horse developed in the English midland 'shires' in medieval times, serving as draught animal and (horrors!) warhorse. The various breeds constitute the largest and heaviest horses in the world, standing up to 19 hands (6ft 4 in) and weighing more than a ton. Here you can see the Suffolk Punch, Clydesdale, and Percheron, as well as several pony breeds: Shetland, Highland, Fell, Dales, Welsh, Exmoor, New Forest, Dartmoor, and Connemara. The West Runton Riding School, based here, is open all year. 01263.837339.

SHERINGHAM

Three thousand years ago, early Britons were living among these rolling hills. Two thousand years ago the Romans built kilns here for firing pottery. Nine hundred years back, Domesday mentioned a church, which was to become **All Saints** in Upper Sheringham.

By 1197 the Augustinian priories at Beeston Regis and **Weybourne** (both now ruined) were serving Walsingham pilgrims, but their main occupation was fishing (ignore the joke about fish friars), with boats launched from the beach. Fish merchants moved here in the 14th century, and Sheringham was born; from 1358 it had a licence to trade with Blakeney.

Sheringham, like Cromer, never had a harbour and was perpetually threatened with coastal erosion, but it prospered nonetheless and in 1452 the church was rebuilt. Then a 16th century tax on all fishing boats working from the village led to detailed records being kept. So we know that in 1591 there were 22 boats, rising to a maximum of some 200, until overcrowding forced some to move to Lincolnshire. We also know that a smokehouse on Wyndham St (*sic*) was probably a storehouse for smugglers.

Inevitably the town turned to boatbuilding – and that led to lifeboats. In 1838 the Hon. Mrs Charlotte Upcher of Sheringham Hall gave the *Augusta*, a 33 ft 16-oar boat named from her daughter. It was stored in a special building on West Cliff from 1838 to 1894, and ended its days on Ranworth Broad. The family's replacement, *Henry Ramey Upcher,* served until 1935, saving around 200 lives. It was last launched to celebrate the defeat of Japan in 1945 and now sits in its old boathouse near West Cliff.

Cromer Lifeboat

The RNLI's old boathouse, built on Lifeboat Plain in 1867, was abandoned after storm damage, and it now holds the §**Sheringham Craft Centre.** The RNLI's present premises are on West Promenade, open to view in summer.

A painting of the *Augusta* is on the wall of the **Two Lifeboats** pub on High Street, the other vessel in the duo being the RNLI's *Duncan.* The pub is almost 300 years old, many of its timbers having come from wrecks. The Upcher family bought the place in 1878 as a coffee house, but it has also been a brothel and a mission-house. Strange mix!

It was the coming of the railway in 1887 which changed the town's destiny. Tourists arrived. People with plenty of money came to *do nothing*, to the locals' amazement. Soon the Sheringham and the Grand hotels were built; the Mainsail Haul began attracting the famous – Vaugn Williams worked on his *Pastoral* here; Captain Robert Falcon Scott and Sir Ernest Shackleton followed. The **drinking fountain** of 1814 became the town reservoir in 1862, and in 1901 a clock was added. It's today's distinctive **Clock Tower**.

In 1842 the Upchers gave the fishermen's chapel, but soon a real church was needed. In 1895 the aldermen laid the foundations of **St Peter's** which was to cost £8,000. Strangely, it didn't become the parish church until 1953 when it was merged with Weybourne.

Do you know Sheringham's odd claim to fame? It was the first town in Britain to be bombed in World War One. A Zeppelin dropped it; it went through the roof of a cottage in Whitehall Yard but never exploded. The occupier carried it away in a bucket.

The town museum opened in 1990 in a fisherman's cottage off Station Road. Open daily in summer, weekends in winter, it has displays of fashion, fishing and local history, with a gift shop. Its neighbour was the home of a washerwoman.

The National Trust owns **Sheringham Park** for details of which please see page 81.

And now for something unusual. A **public lavatory** that is something of a tourist attraction. Go west along the Promenade to the §MARBLE ARCH and see the only loo (unless you know of another) to have stained glass windows.

RESORT RÉSUMÉ. Sheringham is lively without being brash. The beach has some shingle at high tide, but sand lower down. With a few discos, video games, an amusement arcade and Splash, the tropical leisure pool, there is something for everybody. Jet skiing is permitted, subject to restrictions.

§THE POPPY LINE

Sheringham has *two* railway stations, thirty yards apart. *Two?* British Rail closed the line from here to Melton Constable in 1964. At once appeals went out: *join the M&GN Preservation Society!* Response was good but three years passed before the society could buy the three-mile section of line *to* Weybourne, but by then BR had cleared the line *from* Weybourne to Melton Constable and was working steadily west. BR pulled out of Sheringham station in 1967 in favour of a new, smaller, one on the other side of the main road – hence the two stations. So the enthusiasts leased the old one.

93

Over the next twelve years they met continual opposition from a government which despised private enterprise. They formed the North Norfolk Railway Company, raised £14,000 by sale of shares, went to a public inquiry, and finally ran their first steam train in 1976.

The Poppy Line began with two former BR locos: a J15 0-6-0 built at Stratford in 1912; a B12/3 4-6-0 of 1928; *Pony*, an 0-4-0 of 1912; and a series of 0-6-0 configurations: *Fireless*, built in 1929; *Wissington*, used by British Sugar which owned the sugar refinery at Wissington village; a loco from Ashington Colliery; plus *Ringshaw*, *Harlaxton*, and *12*, and an unnamed one from the National Coal Board.

Up to eight trains run daily in each direction in high summer, with the season lasting from April to October.

WEYBOURNE

A pleasant village, Weybourne – which is probably why ex-prime minister Sir John Major chose the hinterland to build his *de luxe* holiday home. It's tucked away out of sight, but §**WEYBOURNE PRIORY** is very much in sight – what's left of it.

The Augustinian canons came to England in the 11th century, building their first priory in Colchester. They arrived in Weybourne by 1216 via West Acre under Sir Roger Meyngaren (now anglicised to Mainwaring or Mannering) whose family held that manor since 1071.

The priory gained some independence in the 14th century but was never big enough to go it alone, despite earning money from pilgrims to Walsingham. Indeed, the Bishop of Norwich noted in 1514 that the place was so poor there was only one canon. By 1530 the prior and canon saw the end was nigh and sold everything in sight except a small crucifix. The next bishop to visit found a priory that had ceased to function even before Henry VIII's bulldozers. The empty buildings, which were collapsing, passed to *Sir John Gresham*, founder of Holt School, and later passed to the Walpole family. All that remain are stone walls 50 feet high, and scars on the ground, the entire complex snucking up to the church's east window.

The Austin canons had earlier absorbed the **church** into their priory and allowed it to collapse in part, and for centuries the parish had neither priest nor usable church: the restoration of the church began in 1866 and was completed by 1888, but for the priory – nothing.

Stand on the low cliffs at Weybourne and look WEST. That part of the coastline is very slowly extending out to sea. Now look EAST: that part is gradually being eroded, right around the littoral until you reach Orford Ness. You are on the very spot where the two great forces of the sea meet, deposition and erosion. In fact, the cliff you are standing on is an indication of the destructive action, for there are no cliffs to the west until you reach Hunstanton. West, the beaches grow to more than a mile wide: east, they are narrow and gritty.

You are at **WEYBOURNE HOPE**, marked on 1940s O.S. maps, where the cutting edge of the south-bound tides has worn a deepish hole in the sea bed. They knew this in the 18th century and recognised the deep water, the beach, and the undefended hinterland as an ideal spot for invasion. Luckily, our enemies didn't know the old rhyme:

He who would Old England win
Must at Weybourne Hope begin.

The first military defences for Weybourne Hope were planned in 1588 with the Spanish Armada on the way, but nothing was done. Artillerymen moved in during the Napoleonic threat, but moved out afterwards.

In 1935 the Army moved in again – and stayed. Gun emplacements, trenches, and barracks formed the *Weybourne Camp* anti-aircraft gunnery school on terminal moraines called the *Muckleburgh Hills*, a mile west of Weybourne. They fired at towed gliders out to sea so often that the Sheringham fishermen complained. Soon the camp was using catapult-launched pilotless aircraft called *drones*, and experimenting with rockets – as ammunition, not targets. Weybourne proved vital to our defences in

Continued on page 98

Continued on page 98

FELBRIGG HALL: National Trust

The Felbrigg family built the first Felbrigg Hall, but the present beautiful Jacobean-style mansion is the work of the Windham family and was begun in 1620. William Windham I planted the chestnuts in the 600-acre park, but it was Wm Windham II who worked on the hall from 1741, after his Grand Tour. He decorated the interior, extended the place to house his paintings, which are still there and form a major feature. The hall also contains 18th century furniture and has an outstanding gothic-style library. It was this William – 'Weathercock' William, who knew which way the political wind blew – who added the mirrors and damask in the main rooms. But it was 'Mad' Windham who went broke in 1863 and had to sell Felbrigg, John Ketton being the buyer. His grandson gave the property to the National Trust in 1970.

The hall offers a magnificent example of a working walled estate garden, with many old varieties and providing fruit and vegetables for visitors to the restaurant: there is also a shop and a second-hand bookshop.

Within the garden are a working dovecote and the National Collection of Colchicums (autumn croci). The park is well-known for its large and agèd trees, and there are many waymarked walks, some passing the church and the lake, while an all-weather path follows the Victory V walk through the woods behind the hall.

Externally, the hall is distinguished by its architecture, with tall windows and chimneys dominating, and the inscription GLORIA DEO IN EXCELSIS being picked out in stonework at parapet level.

The hall is open April to Christmas, with an imaginative programme of events, and the park is open daily, year round, dawn to dusk, thus allowing access to the parish church of St Margaret with work by Grinling Gibbons and monuments to the Felbrigg and Windham families.

Felbrigg Hall

Blickling Hall

BLICKLING HALL: National Trust

Built around 1616 by Sir Henry Hobart, Lord Chief Justice and one of England's great Jacobean houses, Blickling is famed for its spectacular long gallery, superb plasterwork ceilings, and fine collections of furniture, pictures, books and tapestries, including George II's bedhangings in the State Bedroom.

King Harold owned the Blickling lands until losing them to William the Conqueror in 1066. William gave them to Bishop Losinga of Norwich from whom they passed to the Fastolf family.

There is a splendid restaurant, shop, second-hand bookshop, and an exhibition on the RAF at Blickling in WW2, as well as regular art exhibitions. And there is an extensive events programme throughout the year; the hall is open afternoons April to October (not Mon or Tues)

The grounds cover 4,777 acres of wood and farmland, and the gardens are colourful all year, with daffodils, bluebells, azaleas and rhododendrons dominating, with many walks available, from strolls around the lake to longer perambulations. Visitors may also play croquet on the lawn or hire a cycle for a ride around the park and the quiet local roads.

Blickling was home to the Boleyn family, but despite stories to the contrary, Anne Boleyn was born in an earlier hall 109 years before this one was built. Rumour has it that her ghost crosses the elegant front lawns one night early each year. Thomas, Earl of Wiltshire, was the father of Anne and George Boleyn. Anne married Henry VIII in 1532 (some say 1533) and was beheaded in 1536, the last of the Boleyn line.

The Hall eventually passed to the Marquess of Lothian, and the eleventh marquess was Britain's ambassador to the USA when he died in 1940, leaving the entire estate to the National Trust.

WW2, bringing Winston Churchill here in June 1941. Yet the Luftwaffe paid only one visit, in July 1940, when it bombed the camp and the village with no casualties. By the time the last gun was fired in October 1958 – the camp was closed soon after – 250,000 troops had trained here, firing 1,500,000 shells out to sea. But they never filled the hole in the sea bed.

Berry Savory had a military museum in Inveraray Castle, home of the dukes of Argyll, and needed to expand. When he heard that Weybourne Camp was on the market, he bought it, and in May 1988 the Duke of Argyll performed the opening ceremony of what is now:

§The MUCKLEBURGH COLLECTION,

the largest private military collection of its kind in the UK that is open to the public. It started with around 40 military vehicles but now has well over 1,500 exhibits of all kinds, from radio sets and uniforms to working tanks. It is among the most popular visitor attractions in the area covered by this book (competing with Sandringham and Blickling).

The Muckleburgh Collection

The eight exhibition halls were military buildings, including the NAAFI canteen for the original camp. The hardware inside these halls comes from a wide range of countries including several EU states, plus Israel, Norway, Switzerland and the former USSR, and includes the early Willys Jeep, guns, rocket launchers, ambulances, and a diorama of Fighter Command aircrew scrambling to intercept the enemy. Theatres of conflict range from WW2 to the Iraq War, and there are exhibits from the 18th century; a special hall remembers the *Suffolk and Norfolk Yeomanry* founded in 1794 by Viscount Townshend of Raynham.

Tanks are in action at weekends and often daily in summer, and if you want some genuine atmosphere you can listen to music of the war years. Main season is March to November; 01263.588210, or www.muckleburgh.co.uk.

A mile south of the Muckleburgh Hills lies **Kelling**, with a picture gallery – and it's called 'The Gallery' – housed in the old Reading Room built in 1915 by the crossroads.

The old *windmill* east of the village has been restored, but it's now a private home.

GRESHAM

William de Warrenne received the Gresham estates soon after the Norman Conquest. Under Henry II the village received its charter for a market, but it did not grow: maybe it was too close to Sheringham as it was only three miles south. The lack of development saved **All Saints' Church** so it still has its §**Saxon round tower**.

Edmund Bacon, squire of Gresham, built a fortified manor in 1319 which became Gresham Castle and which the **Paston** family (see later) bought in 1429. A Lord Moleyns besieged it when squire John Paston was away in London, and managed to evict Mrs Paston and the servants. Soon after, the Pastons abandoned the place and now only a few ruins remain.

The GRESHAMS came to prominence in the 14th century. Two centuries later, Sir Thomas G. was a merchant and financial adviser to Henry VIII, Mary, and Elizabeth. It was he who established the **Royal Exchange** in London, which opened in 1571. It was he who introduced the symbol of the **locust** to the world of finance and, years later, it became the logo of Martin's Bank, taken over in the 1970s by Barclays. The insect is still seen at Gresham's School. But our interest is in Thomas's brother, **Sir John**, who moved to Holt: remember the name.

As you leave Gresham westwards for Holt, you may notice an isolated church at a crossroads and find yourself in a vanished village: North Barningham. Go west and you reach **Baconsthorpe**, whose name means the village of the Bacon family. The font of St Mary's Church, presented in 1888, began sinking, and a search revealed a coffin under the floor: the coffin belonged to the Bacon family. Now look in the centre of the roof for a shield bearing an M (for Mary) and three *pigs'* heads. The same heads appear in stained glass in the south windows, taken from §**Baconsthorpe Castle** in 1958 to repair bomb damage.

Yet the name most prominent in the church is Heydon, a family which had vast sheep holdings in Tudor times. The Heydons' coat of arms is the engrailed cross seen on the monument blocking a window in the south aisle.

At the eastern end of Gresham village on Sustead Road is the **Young's Pot Shop** which sells its wares around the world. The business specialises in brown and green earthenware and has more than 20 years' trading experience.

Now back to the Heydons. John of that ilk was a lawyer with a reputation for cheating, so when he fortified the family house and wool-processing factory and converted them into Baconsthorpe Castle, he never applied for the royal say-so. Family fortunes were low by 1600 and after the Civil Wars of 1642-'49 most of the castle was demolished. The gatehouse survived 200 years as Baconsthorpe Hall; the courtyard struggled on as a walled garden, but only a vestige remains. English Heritage owns it with no restriction on entry. I find it interesting as a great anachronism and industrial relic in rural Norfolk.

Lady Jane Grey, queen for 13 days in July 1553, was related to Thomas and Jane de Grey, who were orphaned in 1562. Both were made wards of Queen Elizabeth and sent, as children, to *Baconsthorpe*, where they died. That's the true story, but it has been bowdlerised a bit and is now well-known as the tale of THE BABES IN THE WOOD.

HOLT and GRESHAM'S SCHOOL

WHEN SIR JOHN GRESHAM (remember him?) arrived in Holt in 1546, he bought the Manor House for £170 and converted it into a school for the sole purpose of teaching boys grammar: a true 'grammar' school. He endowed the school with land in 12 parishes, and houses in Cripplegate, London. In October 1556 he appointed the 'Wardens of the Mistery (*sic*) of Fishmongers' as governors, and a week later he died of the plague.

The school opened in 1562 for 30 scholarship boys, plus fee-payers. Almost all teachers were ordained churchmen (the only citizens who could write?) who needed a licence from the bishop, who therefore controlled the curriculum, and made 'visitations' to check it.

Thomas Tallis, headmaster in 1606, made Gresham's school one of the best in the area, sending 24 boys to Caius College, Cambridge, during his 34 years in office. And he left his private library to the school.

A Royalist uprising in Holt in 1650, the year after Charles I lost his head, showed mass opposition to Cromwell. On Christmas Day 25 Royalists were executed at Norwich, including Thomas Cooper, an usher at the school, but local legend claims he was really the headmaster and he was hanged at the school.

Timber and thatch houses have always been a fire risk. On Mayday 1708 most of the town burned down, causing damage worth £20,000; the fire travelled so fast, it was said, that nobody could save the meat from the market stalls. The thatched chancel of the church blazed, and molten lead from the nave burned holes in the stone floor – the signs are still there. Gresham's School escaped with minor damage, and the rebuilt town moved a little to the west.

In 1792 John Holmes was appointed headmaster. Holmes, who was *not* a churchman, added geography and history to the curriculum, and when he didn't like existing textbooks he wrote his own. The next head was a preacher, and became vicar of Sheringham and Weybourne while still ruling the school. The divided loyalty showed: two rival schools opened in Holt, taking most of his pupils. A new lay head had to work hard, adding arithmetic, geometry, Latin and Greek – but his successors were still churchmen.

Then came Mr Howson. Given the headship in 1900, in 19 years he transformed a lacklustre school with 44 boys into a public school of national appeal. He added science, French, and German; he abolished the cane; he had new buildings, the nucleus of the present school. But most of all he turned the institution into Gresham's *School*, without alienating the people of Holt who wanted it to keep its local character.

By 1988 Sir John Gresham's school was charging £7,275 a year each for 470 senior boarders (plus 200 at prep) and employing a staff of 225 who were paid a total of £2,000,000 a year. In many respects, Gresham's School *is* Holt.

The fire destroyed much of interest in the town, although Holt's quaint street plan and many old and mock-old buildings

101

remain, giving the place character. But §**St Andrew's Church** suffered only roof damage, which didn't disturb the pipistrelle bats which breed in the nave nor the jackdaws in the tower.

There's lots more nature to be seen in the 100-acre **Holt Country Park** 10 minutes' walk south of the town.

LETHERINGSETT

The large, brick water mill at Letheringsett was built around 1800 at a time when there were 508 such mills in Norfolk. This is now the sole survivor. The Domesday record mentions 'Leringaseta,' and other records tell of John de Keyly and William de Gatele buying 48 acres *and a watermill*. By 1720 John Brereton owned the mill, the house, which became Letheringsett Hall, and a brewery. The mill burned down but was rebuilt by 1754; it burned again in 1800 and was again rebuilt. The supply of water to the millpond had been agreed in 1765, but in 1945 a diesel engine replaced water power and so the place was a watermill no longer. But the millstones remained and since the discerning public now wanted fine white flour, not coarse stone-ground stuff, the mill closed.

Restoration began in 1987 using the original water-wheel and without any grant, and §**Letheringsett Mill** is again in business, producing 3½ tons of flour a week, most sold on the premises for animal and pet food. It's *open* on select afternoons in summer.

The round tower of the village **church** was built after Domesday, but is pure Saxon in style, with 15th-century windows. In 1236 a local man had given land to Binham Priory which, in return, built the rest of the church; the prior of Binham appointed priests from 1308 to 1422.

In 1786 John Burrell, son-in-law of Mr Holmes, Gresham's headmaster, was rector, giving free reign to his love of insects. Burrell sold most of the estate to William Hardy who was mad on trees and – as his epitaph states – *clothed these once-barren hills with foliage*. And probably helped feed Burrell's insects. Keble College, Oxford, now holds the patronage.

Look at the tombstone just inside the churchyard. Johnson Jex taught himself the art of watchmaking, but first had to teach himself French in order to read a book on the subject. He made every tool he needed, and even engraved this inside a watch he made:

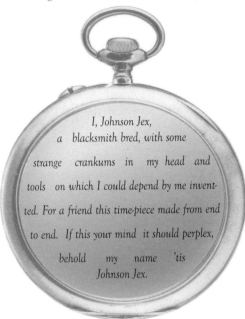

I, Johnson Jex,
a blacksmith bred, with some
strange crankums in my head and
tools on which I could depend by me invent-
ted. For a friend this time-piece made from end
to end. If this your mind it should perplex,
behold my name 'tis
Johnson Jex.

BAYFIELD is another vanishing village. There's only the Hall and the ivy-clad skeleton of the church, which was abandoned in 1927. Its last patron was none other than Sir Alfred Joddrell who built Glandford Church.

The Felbrigg Family built the first Felbrigg Hall, but it now belongs to the National Trust. For information on the house, **see page 96.**

MISCELLANY

South from Felbrigg there's Andrew and Joanna Young's **Pottery** at Lower Gresham, who have samples of their stoneware in the V&A.

Ancient St Mary the Virgin at **Roughton** has a short Saxon tower. **Thurgarton**'s thatched All Saints' had a Saxon tower until its collapse in 1882, but St Mary's at **Aldborough** has Saxon puddingstone masonry in the nave; neither church has a tower. **Thwaite**'s round tower is Norman; St Ethelbert's at **Alby** has Saxon remains but the main interest is the rood stairs.

In the village, call at **Alby Crafts** on the crossroads. Linda Matthews has restored farm buildings to hold studios producing a range of crafts in textiles, pottery, woodwork, graphic art; they change from time to time.

Our Lady and St Margaret's at **Calthorpe** has a north-facing Devil's door and a corbel with two female faces, one of them gagged. **Erpingham's** Church of St Mary has a tall tower, and a font rescued from St Benedict's in Norwich, a victim of WW2 bombs. See the brass of Sir John de Erpingham whose son Thomas built the Erpingham Gate at Norwich Cathedral. St Lawrence's at **Ingworth** lost its Saxon round tower in 1822 so the stump is thatched to match the nave roof.

Wolterton Hall, west of Calthorpe, was built for Horace Walpole between 1727 and 1741. It was abandoned in 1858 in favour of **Mannington Hall**, which was badly damaged by fire in 1952. Following the death of the owner, Lord Walpole, in 1989, the new Lord and Lady Walpole began major restoration at Wolterton, which is now open during the tourist season. Phone 01263.584175 for information on both places.

§AYLSHAM

This small market town, called Elesham in the Domesday Book, has an unspoiled centre based on the Buttlands, once the home of archery butts where townsmen were obliged to practice shooting arrows until the 18th century; it's now a car park. Look for the charming Black Boy Inn in Queen Anne style, the 17th century Manor House, Old Hall, and The Knoll.

The town was first recorded around the Norman Conquest when Brithric was the Saxon priest and William the Conqueror held the manor. From 1087 Battle Abbey appointed the priest and collected the tithes, but Henry VIII sent the tithes to Canterbury after he sacked Battle.

Aylsham was a prominent wool and linen town: in 1327 Edward II bought 3,500 ells of 'Aylleshamme'. (One ell is 45 inches.) John of Gaunt, father of Henry IV, became manorial lord of Aylsham in 1372 and when Gaunt died in 1399 Henry merged the Crown with the Duchy of Lancaster, making Aylsham the main town in Norfolk for the Lancastrians. Later, Sir Thomas Erpingham became lord of the manor and influenced affairs of the church. Then the lordship passed to Charles I who mortgaged it to the City of London, defaulted, and saw the manor pass to Sir John Hobart of Blickling Hall.

Legend claims Edward III chose the site of §St **Michael and All Angels'** church, the oldest building in town, but the Victorian influence is strong, as the remaining old box pews show, looking like an old-style railway carriage. But come here any Monday lunch-time, May to October, for a concert.

Probably the best-known resident of the cemetery is Humphry Repton, who died in 1818, the landscape gardener who was second only to Capability Brown.

Under Queen Mary, when England again saw the Pope as the head of the Church, John Bury, Vicar of Aylsham, condemned glovemaker Thomas Hudson as a heretic and had him burned at the stake in Norwich. Bury is mentioned in Fox's *Book of Martyrs* as a very evil man...a great swearer, given to women, persecuting the gospel and compelling men to idolatry.

Clare and Robert Hoare swapped a lawn mower for six black Welsh Mountain sheep in 1966. They keep the more than 1,000 descendants at Ingworth where the fleece is harvested to supply the knitwear factory of **Black Sheep**, Ltd, in Penfold St, Aylsham.

§BURE VALLEY RAILWAY

The Bure Valley Railway (BVR) is a joint venture between Broadland District Council and the BVR Company. In 1978 Norfolk County Council and BDC bought the track-bed from Norwich north-west to Attlebridge and established the Marriott's Way footpath. They later bought the bed from Lenwade (near Attlebridge, see the chapter on railways) to Hoveton, by Wroxham. Norfolk council took the sector from Lenwade to Aylsham for another path, while the district council took the Aylsham to Wroxham bit. Council and rail company have together developed the BVR and – since the gauge is only fifteen inches – a 'Huff and Puff' cycle path beside it, all costing £2,500,000 financed by the English Tourist Board and the D of E.

The first locomotives were leased from the Romney, Hythe & Dymchurch Railway, later joined by locos from Ravenglass & Eskdale, and Bressingham Gardens. The fledgling company changed hands several times, once being put into receivership, but the present owner is Westernasset Ltd.

The new track has 17 bridges, over or under, a long culvert under the Aylsham bypass, and a bridge over the Bure at Buxton, the central of three stations.

At one point the line curves to go around the end of the runway of **RAF Coltishall**, sometime home of 242 Squadron, commanded by legless Sqn. Ldr Douglas Bader. Spitfires flew from here before the USAAF moved in, hence one loco is called *Spitfire*, although in recent times Jaguars used the base. Other locos are *Wroxham Broad, Thunder, Little Titan, Count Louis*, and a diesel called *2nd Air Division USAAF* (yes, really!) And there's one called *Blickling Hall*.

For a description of the National Trust property of Blickling Hall**, see page 97.**

The Blickling estate's stubby-towered Church of St Andrew is mainly 15th century but has numerous brasses. There's one to Nicholas de Dagworth, builder of the first hall; to *Anna* Boleyn who died in 1479; to Roger and Cecily Felthorp with their ten sons and six daughters; and to others.

The COAST to HAPPISBURGH

Down the A149, **Thorpe Market** has a towerless church, built in 1795-'96 in mock Gothic, but **Southrepps** has a traditional church with a tower 114 ft high, and was as big as a cathedral before it lost its aisles in 1791. **Trimingham** has its Church of St John the Baptist's *Head*, a bizarre dedication supporting belief that the severed head was actually here. People even came on pilgrimage to see it.

William de Warrenne was lord of the manor of **Gimingham** as well as founder of the Cluniac Priory at Lewes, Sussex, which still appoints the parsons here. The thatched Church of St Nicholas at **Swafield** shows the saint with his three bags of gold. **Trunch**'s Church of St Botolph survived the Puritanic purge of 1643 because the chancel was used as a schoolroom; see the initials scratched on the walls. **Knapton** has one of England's best double-hammerbeam roofs, made from Irish oak in 1503. Legend claims it was cargo in a wrecked ship. **Antingham** is an oddity; the ruins of the 12th century church are beside the still-used St Mary's Church, where the brass to Richard Calthorpe shows him with his nineteen children.

And so to **WORSTEAD**. This tiny village was so important in medieval times that it gave its name to a type of cloth. The village is a collection of pleasant houses around a market square, and

Geoffrey the Dyer's House is named from Geoffrey Litester who led the local Peasants' Revolt against the poll tax. Yet he never lived in this house!

§**St Mary's Church**, begun in 1379, is big enough to hold the entire parishioners several times over, a testimony to the importance of wool. The tower is 109 ft tall but, inside, you are awed by the vast size, the box pews and the hammerbeam roof. St Mary's Guild of Weavers, Spinners, and Dyers keeps a §**museum** of the days of glory, showing wool samples and how to weave the material which is still popular for men's suits.

MUNDESLEY

William Cowper spent his last years (1795-1800) between Mundesley and East Dereham. Cowper, best known for his poem *John Gilpin*, was suffering from depression and eventually quit Mundesley because he didn't like the east wind.

The village, pronounced 'Munzly', was called Muleslai in Domesday, and made its living from fishing. The railway's arrival in 1898 brought tourists, who still come despite the railway's departure in 1964. The Royal Hotel claims that Horatio Nelson stayed there while he studied at North Walsham.

It had a lifeboat from 1811 to 1895; under its cox William Withers the boat saved six men on 17 November 1868 then went out the next day and saved the entire crew from another ship. A bomb was erected in the town centre in 2004 as a memorial to soldiers and civilians killed by mines on the beach during and after the war.

Mundesley sits on a vein of clay which provided material for most of its bricks, but the last trace of the industry is the office at the Kiln Cliffs Caravan Park; it's an old kiln.

All Saints' Church, a towerless modern renovation of a 14th century ruin, had two nototious rectors in Tudor times. John Russell was a part-time poacher, and James Matchett was a minor criminal, often in court.

Mundesley today offers quiet beach holidays; the sands are moderately wide and accommodation ranges from smart hotel to caravan. Tourist office: Station Road, 01263.721070.

South of the village is §**Stow Mill**, built in 1827 and abandoned in the 1930s. Mike Newton bought it in 1971 and has restored it. It's open daily, and leave your donation in the box.

PASTON and BACTON

The tiny village of Paston owes its limited fame to the Paston family who corresponded with the leaders of society from 1422 to 1509 – *and kept copies of the originals and their replies.* The **Paston Letters** are among the earliest surviving texts in English, and offer an intriguing insight into life in those times The Pastons kept the letters as a family record, but when the last in line, William Paston, Earl of Yarmouth, died in 1732, the records were sold. A Diss chemist bought them, sold them on to John Fenn of Dereham, who published them in stages. This letter was written in 1425, the Þ (þ in old English font) being an early form of *th* as in 'the':

To my well beloued John Staynford of Furnyvales Inne.

To enquerre and wyte whether þe stoon may be sawed or nought, and whether it wille chip or chynne or affraye with frost of weder or water.

Al-so þat euery pece of þe stoon be iij foote longe and þat xv tunne tygh... [lost] ... of þe stoon be euery weel bedded into þe walle and a foote thikke þat it ryse in heighte a foote in þe walle..

I'd better put that in understandable type:

To my well beloued John Staynford of Furnyvales Inne.

To enquerre and wyte [wit = know] whether Þe stoon may be sawed or nought [not], and whether it wille chippe or chynne or affraye with frost of weder [weather] or water.

Al-so Þat euery pece of Þe stoon be iij foote longe and Þat xv tunne tygh… [lost] …of Þe stoon be euery weel bedded into Þe walle and a foote thikke Þat it ryse in heighte a foote in Þe walle…

Difficult, isn't it? In 1464 the first John Paston petitioned Edward IV to urge him to make certain appointments to the church, and in only 40 years the Þ character had gone. It's still found in Icelandic, and even in the Third Reich, German used to be printed in script.

To the Kyng owre sovereyn Lord

Please it powre Highnes to graunte vn-to powre humble seruant John Paston the older, squire, powr gracious letters patentz of licence to fownde, stabilysh, and endewe in the gret mancion of

Castre be Mekyll Yermowth (Caister by Great [Muckle = much] Yarmouth) in Norffolk, that late was John Fastolffes, knight, cosyn to powre seyd beseecher, a colage of vj prystes.

There are numerous mentions of the Pastons in the thatched church of St Margaret, but the most imposing monument is the enormous §**Paston Barn** built in 1581 in a neighbouring field. This is a tourist attraction yet to be exploited.

...BACTON

East of the barn we get back to modern times with the **Bacton Gas Terminal**. The Dutch struck methane two miles down in 1959, and Britain found its own reserves in 1965 in the West Sole Field, piped ashore in Holderness. But our biggest fields – Leman, Hewett, Dottie Deborah and others – lay off Norfolk. The receiving terminal you see here behind wire fences, covers 200 acres and can handle four thousand million cubic feet a day. But you could drive by and not notice it. A chimney was planned, to burn off 'sour gas', and you would have noticed *that*, for miles around.

South of Bacton are the ruins of **Bromholm Priory**, to which Henry III once walked, barefoot.

A HAPPISBURGH farewell

Our journey ends in a place that should be cheerful – Happisburgh. But it's not happy at all due to severe erosion. So let's call it by its phonetic name, **Hazebr'.** William the Conqueror gave the manor to Roger Bigod, of the family which produced the dukes of Norfolk, but when William d'Albini, head of the royal household, married Bigod's daughter Maud, he received Happisburgh as a dowry. Albini built Castle Rising, founded a priory which was to become Wymondham Abbey, and gave Happisburgh to the priory's first abbot.

In the 14th century the Norman church was demolished to make way for the present structure, its tower to serve as a landmark for 500 years along a dangerous stretch of coast, for the Happisburgh Sands are not far offshore and the sea has eternally been Hazebr's nemesis.

Daniel Defoe, author of Robinson Crusoe, saw the sea's menace in 1724 when he commented on the number of ships' timbers used in barns and houses. Despite the tower helping navigation, the churchyard holds hundreds of shipwreck victims, including a mass grave for 119 seamen from HMS *Invincible*, proved to be very vincible in March 1801.

Two lighthouses were here when the warship went down; one was demolished late in the 19th century. But when Trinity House announced in June 1988 that it wanted to decommission the remaining light, local people objected. Within a month the Happisburgh Lighthouse Trust was formed, but it learned that only Trinity House may operate a lighthouse. The NatWest Bank paid the £15,000 that was needed to get a new Act through Parliament, and in August 1990 the trust began running Britain's only private working lighthouse.

But for how long? This village has hit the national news on several occasions for one very nasty reason. It is eroding. Each winter many yards of soft cliff tumble into the sea; each year another house or more must be abandoned to the waves. We have seen the demise of Godwick far inland, but Happisburgh will disappear just as surely. In Suffolk, Dunwich went long ago, as did Walton Castle by Felixstowe. We cannot stop the land encroaching seawards at Scolt Head or Blakeney; neither can we stop the sea encroaching landwards along this strip of coast. It is merely a matter of time, and we all know that time and tide wait for no man.

Boats and beaches are a feature of north Norfolk.

Index to placenames